SCARLET HILTIBIDAL

HE NUMBERED

THE PORES ON MY FACE

HOTTIE LISTS, CLOGGED PORES,
EATING DISORDERS, AND
FREEDOM FROM IT ALL

B&H
PUBLISHING
Nashville, Tennessee

Dedicated to Ever, Brooklyn (Dewy), and Joy, my favorite girls with the most beautiful pores ever created

Disclaimer: All names have been changed, because no thirty-three-year-old man needs to be called out in a book for telling me my hair looked like it got run over by a lawn mower twenty years ago. I forgive you, *"Kent."* I fully forgive you.

CONTENTS

Section 3:
The Gospel Tells You Who You'll Be

INTRODUCTION

I used to stare at my own face in the mirror for fun.

I would lock my tween-age self in the bathroom of our two-story condo in Burbank, sit on top of the bathroom sink, and get as close as I could to the mirror, studying each pore as if I had to have their precise layout memorized by the next day. I'd sit, and I'd study, and I'd whisper. Softly, as I perused my pores, I would recite the speech I was going to give my crush when he finally said, "Scarlet . . . I love you, and I always have."

I imagined that when he told me that, on our last day of seventh grade, under a tree with just the right number of leaves to let in a romantically speckled amount of sunlight, I would be wearing a flower crown and a diamond anklet and a calmly radiant smile, like Mona Lisa. My response would be something like, "I love you too. I've loved you since the moment I saw you drawing UFOs on the paper bag cover of your earth science book in Ms. Chang's class. Also, you have handsome pores."

I practiced that speech, but I never got to deliver it.

My mirror-proximity problem had a lot to do with the fact that I grew up with a very blonde, very blue-eyed, and quite famous mother. She got a lot of positive attention everywhere we went. I looked nothing like her. But something in me said that if only I looked like my beautiful, fawned-over mom, I would be happy. *Get it together, Scarlet. Be beautiful.*

I tried. At twelve, I wasn't allowed to dye my hair yet, so I squeezed lemons onto it and sat outside in direct sunlight. I'd read in *Seventeen* magazine that lemon juice made hair turn blonde. I remember desperately sprinting indoors to see if I was blonde and beautiful and ready to be famous. I wasn't. I was just weirdly sunburned. Those were brutal years of daily battles. No matter how many lemons I crushed, no matter how many pores I pondered, no matter how many articles I read, I pretty much always looked like this.

By the way, when I texted my sister, asking if she could track down a photo of me during my awkward stage, that photo came through in a matter of seconds, as if she already had it set as her home screen or something.

Anyway, I guess I'm an adult now? I'm the age I thought was old when I was a teenager. But I'm wearing a romper right now. Does that mean I'm still young? I say the answer is yes.

Okay, so why is this oldish lady writing a book about her younger days? Well, because I have daughters who will check their pores soon. And I'm watching teen girls all around me growing up and growing scared and wondering if they are enough.

I see them. I recognize the look in their eyes and the hopes in their hearts.

I look around and I see it. My oldest daughter is pretty confident, and she's suffered no shortage of compliments in her eight years. But even as young as four, when her baby sister was born, I could already see the twinge of hurt wash over her face when people complimented her little sister's bright-blue eyes. I could already see the wheels turning as she tried to decipher the meaning behind her brown eyes, as she listened to a convincing internal voice, for maybe the first time in her life, whispering, *You're not as beautiful as you should be. You're not as special as you could be.*

I don't want these girls—this beautiful, bubbly generation of young women—to waste years trying to look different, trying to be adored by the wrong people, and trying to accomplish stuff that looks like everything but feels like nothing. Instead, there's a real freedom and deep peace already sitting there from Jesus. That freedom eluded me when I was a teen. It's something I'm just now starting to grasp, thirty-plus years into this life.

My adopted daughter, Joy, was born without ears. She's only five, but she's starting to notice the sparkles in the ears of girls around her. She picks earrings out of my jewelry dish and holds them up to her head. Then she slips

3

on a twenty-nine-cent necklace, smiles into the mirror, and signs "beautiful" to herself. Even at five, she longs to be admired.

But no matter how many times I tell my oldest that I want to eat her beautiful brown eyes up like milk chocolate kisses, or how many times I show Joy that a sparkly necklace is beautiful, just like a sparkly earring, their deceitful little hearts aren't going to be able to ignore the crushing messages the whole wide world will offer them.

You're not enough unless you're this . . .
You can't be happy unless you buy this/wear this/
have this/look like this . . .
If you can't do this, you might as well give up
now . . .

That's a problem. That's an everyday, every-girl, soul-level problem.

So, what can help? What can fix it?

Certainly not me.

I can't save any of you from being broken humans. From chasing the wrong things. From believing lies. From having broken hearts that betray. From falling and crying and hurting. I wish I could. I look at my daughters and the teen girls at my church and the teens I pass at Target, and I wish I could force hope into female hearts. I can't.

But I can share what helped me. What made me finally settled and joyful and more hopeful than not. I (almost) never stare at my pores anymore. And it's not because I fixed all my problems. It's not because my pores have magically improved over the past twenty years.

Listen: I'm still not pretty enough, or accomplished enough, or popular enough for my heart to be happy. And I don't think I've ever really found self-esteem. Peace doesn't come because I learned to love myself. There are plenty of reasons not to love me. But you know what?

I am loved.

Not by a guy with relatively little acne. Not by friends who think I'm smart or fun or (fill in the blank). Not even by myself. Those loves are weak loves. Like many have said before me, I am loved, as are you, by the One who said that you are so broken that someone had to die for you, but you are so treasured that He did.

We are loved by Jesus, the One who made us, the One who rescued us, the One who wants to be with us forever. When we understand who we already are—forgiven and loved daughters of God—because of what Jesus already did on the cross, who we haven't dated and what we haven't done are insignificant.

Your identity, or who you are, is not tied up in what you look like or what you've done or what you'll do. You are a girl who Jesus loves. That's your identity.

Your identity, or who you are, is not tied up in what you look like or what you've done or what you'll do. You are a girl who Jesus loves. That's your identity.

5

I pray that you who have found this book will grow up to find the answers to your search for security and beauty and self-worth in what Jesus has already made true in you.

My seventh-grade mind told me that a flower crown and some confidence would make me beautiful and happy. But even then, God was pursuing. Even then, He was helping me to see who He died for me to be.

The sooner your heart switches from seeking self-worth to seeing what Jesus says you're worth, the sooner you will experience what you long for—that easy, carefree smile you see on the girl by the lockers who seems to have everything she wants and needs. She doesn't, actually. But she can. And so can you. Because—get this—everything you want and need really is found in Christ.

As we fumble our way through each day, falling and failing and trying again to make our lives more centered on a crown of life than on a crown of flowers (see James 1:12; Revelation 2:10), I pray that God will continue to transform us from the little girls we all often are into mature women whose eyes are looking not to a mirror that tells us what we look like, but to a Savior who tells us who we are.

Section 1

THE GOSPEL REDEFINES WHO YOU WERE

Chapter 1

THE HOTTIE LIST

In 1999, my dad found "The Hottie List" under my mattress. It was a well-thought-out ranking of the eighteen hotties I went to school with on the basis of cuteness, dreaminess, and how likely I felt they were to fall in love with me. The conclusion at the bottom was a succinct exclamation.

"Ayyyeeeeeee! I just love boys soooooooo much!"

Three things:

1. The "Ayyyeeeeeee!" was because I lived in Miami. *Note: If you didn't know, Miami is roughly 99.9 percent Hispanic. "Aye!" is kind of like saying "Oh man!" or "Wow!"*

2. Yes, that was a real sentence I wrote on a real list of real boys' names that I still remember.

3. The list was buried in my bed and, had the world been fairer and had my dad been

a less thorough bed-maker, would have stayed buried in my bed forever.

You see, I had this complex about growing up. I felt guilty and ashamed that I was starting to like boys. Ranking hotties, for whatever reason, was a secret so classified that it had to remain hidden in my heart and under my mattress.

When I got home from school that day and heard my dad say, "Scarlet, I was changing the sheets, and I found . . . ," I instantly collapsed into a puddle and let out a sound very similar to a whale noise option on a sound machine app.

I knew what was under those sheets. I now knew that he knew what was under those sheets. We both knew that I had a list, and that it was a list full of hotties.

(Whale whimper)

I spent what felt like the rest of the evening, but was probably more like ten minutes, sobbing weakly in the corner of my messy closet. I had my little sister bring me two slices of Papa John's at dinnertime because I was hungry but too devastated to emerge from my corner of mismatched socks and outgrown shoes.

We both knew that I had a list, and that it was a list full of hotties.

Why did I have such icky feelings about my hottie list? I think part of it was that it all felt so far-fetched—the idea that any of the eighteen hotties I listed could ever feel the same way about me. Or even close to it. But mostly I didn't want anyone on earth to know that I had thirteen-year-old-who-won't-be-named ranked ahead of another thirteen-year-old-who-won't-be-named, simply because one time he accidentally (but maybe not too accidentally) bumped into me in line at the lunchroom, and that seemed like a really right way to start a life together.

Hotties All Over the USA

I grew up going to elementary school with the same seventy-five-ish kids in Miami until seventh grade, when my mom moved us back to Los Angeles for her job. I thought my class was pretty small compared to classes down the street that schooled kids my age by the thousands. But this new school in LA, well, let me put it this way: there were two boys in my grade and eight girls. We were a class of only ten humans. There was a very distinct "popular group" and a clearly noticeable "outsider" cluster. I was immediately well loved by members of the less cool cluster and by my English teacher, Mr. Chapman.

Also, because the boys were scarce, my hottie list was pretty short that year.

I really liked this one boy—let's call him Johnny—but he was too cute and too sweet and too talented and just generally too out of my league to even waste hottie list space on (though that didn't stop me from reciting my "I love you too" speech in my mirror with him in mind. If you'd like to revisit the speech, flip back to the intro). He was a drummer, and he had impossibly bright-blue eyes. Well-liked by the populars, he was also kind to the cluster. My approach with him was basically just to try not to take every kind gesture he directed my way as a marriage proposal.

But I didn't stop with Johnny. I decided to add another out-of-my-league guy to the list. Due to the shortage and unattainability of the (two) boys in my grade, I started observing boys in other grades. Well, one boy. He was a boy a year ahead of me; I'll call him Jamie (but that's not his name either). I remember his real name, of course, and his spiky hair. He hung out with the populars in my grade and his. Tragically, I was caught in the cluster.

Something you also need to know about this period of time is that a movie called *Clueless* was a thing. The main character, Cher, was blonde and pretty and cool (I mean, duh; her name was Cher—more on the importance of names and popularity in chapter 9), and when guys liked her, she'd roll her eyes and flip her hair and say things like, "Ugh! As if!" or "What-ever!" while making a *W* with her fingers.

To an oldest child with no real gauge on what teen romance was supposed to look like other than hearing the lyrics of Celine Dion (she was the Adele of my day) songs, my brain told me that whatever Cher said to boys who liked her was the cool, acceptable, and appropriate response.

The problem was, I wasn't cool, and by most teen guy standards, I wasn't pretty either. But I didn't know that yet. I just knew what Cher would do.

So, one day, I was walking up the outdoor stairwell to get to my next class when none other than Jamie himself, in all his spike-haired splendor, came up behind me and said, "Scarlet, will you go out with me?"

He couldn't see my face, which I'm sure had a huge smile plastered on it. I was too excited to be right in the middle of what I thought was my first romantic experience to notice that he and his friends were already giggling when I swung my head around and barked, in total Cher-from-*Clueless* fashion, "GO OUT WITH YOU? UGH! AS IF!"

This is a true story.

But somewhere between the "ugh" and the "AS IF," I read the room and realized I wasn't being asked out at all. I was being made fun of.

Humiliation is just not a fun feeling at all. When you think you're being flattered and realize you're the butt of the joke, it's completely the WORST. And when it happens during your Cher impression, it is somehow more the worst. And it opens your heart up to believing some pretty terrible lies.

Hottie-Rejection-Induced Lies

The whole "Ugh! As if!" incident made a string of questions start looping in my head, every day, all the time. I'm not sure if these crippling questions had been there before,

but after the Jamie joke crushed my heart, I crawled back
to my cluster, and the questions came continually.

Am I ugly?

Am I weird?

Am I a joke?

Why am I a joke?

Do I need more eyebrow scrunch on my "AS IF!"?

What am I doing wrong?

Am I doing anything right?

What do the cool girls have that I don't?

*Why do I get the trendy things exactly one second after
they stop being cool, every time, without fail?*

Will I ever be pretty?

How does someone get pretty?

Will I ever be admired?

Will I ever be loved?

Our hearts have a natural enemy (remember that mean,
convincing voice we talked about in the introduction?), and
he loves it when our inner monologue is full of lies. His
name is Satan. He is real, and he *loves* these questions. You've
probably already heard them. You've probably already asked
them. He loves to prey on girls in middle school, high school,
college, and even women in their thirties and beyond, caus-
ing us to question whether or not we are loved.

> Our hearts have a natural enemy, and he loves it when our inner monologue is full of lies.

He especially loves to get us thinking about our past mistakes.

Our enemy wants us to feel unloved, and then he wants us to spend every moment of the rest of our lives remembering the moment we believed those lies with our whole hearts.

He wants to lead us into horrible moments of humiliation, regret, and sin, and then bring our minds back to those moments over and over like a playlist on repeat. He wants us to set up a tent and live there. Because if we live there, we are crippled. If we live there, we are slaves.

The First Lies

Have you heard of the first girl who ever lived? Her name was Eve.

Please fight the urge to skim over this part because you've heard/read/seen the story a dozen/hundred/thousand times.

Listen: I'm with you. I've heard it countless times as well. I know that Eve's story can easily become this kind of bogus-sounding tale you feel detached from. Like, *Yeah, she was this old lady who talked to a snake and ate fruit and ruined everything and hid in a shrub and messed everything up for the rest of us, who would have totally preferred living in a perfect garden.*

But let's just think about this on a more personal level.

Before Eve was a sinner and a snake-talker and a fruit-eater, she was just a girl. The first one. Eve had no other girls to compare herself to on Instagram. Because there were no other girls. And there was no Instagram. Can you even *imagine* that life?

And God loved this one and only girl fully and completely. And she walked with Him, and He told her and showed her, through the blessing of a perfect world and friendship with Him, that she was loved and she was special. With His acts and His words, God showed this first girl that she could trust Him. *I have created you so that we can be together, and I'm giving you and this first boy everything I've made.*

But soon, even with no other girls around, with no Netflix or social media feeds, she started hearing other words. The enemy of her heart was there at the beginning with lies that have been told since the very beginning. She heard those little lies and the sly doubts and questions that the enemy planted in her heart. . . . *Does God really love you? Is He really faithful and true? Are you missing out on something better? Are you not good enough?*

Eve doubted her Maker and questioned her value and chose to sin in hopes that she would become something more. Something enough. She ate the fruit, trying to quiet the questions, and she changed the course of the world.

She and that first boy brought sin into the world, which brought with it pain, evil, suffering, doubts, hopelessness, insecurity, loneliness, and so many tears. Ultimately, her sin fractured her perfect relationship with her Creator, the one thing that would have really made her happy.

And like the many ailments and tendencies we have inherited from our parents and grandparents, a sin-infused nature has also been passed down to every single one of us. We continue to cry over the pain that sin brought with it. The questions have carried over. The lies have lasted a really long time.

We believe the lies of mean guys and mean girls and a sinister enemy because we were born with hearts that distrust God. We were born chasing things that lead to death and running from the only One who knows how to perfectly love us.

It's all right there in our origin story. In Genesis 3, the first recorded words of Satan are, "Did God really say, 'You can't eat from any tree in the garden'?" (v. 1).

Satan is so evil and shifty. He didn't flat-out say the lie. He made Eve consider it herself. He set the stage for HER to birth the lie.

Maybe for you, it starts out something like, *Is what that girl said about me true?*

Maybe that lie leads to *Am I really worth anything?*

And maybe that lie leads to *Is there something I can do to get what God isn't giving me?*

And paying attention to those lies and doubts leads to actions that are sinful, which ultimately separates you from the only One who can give you joy and peace inside. The only One who can really tell you who you are.

Maybe you join your peers as they make fun of the quiet girl who always eats lunch by herself, and that makes you feel like you fit in for a second, but then you remember that God's Word says, "Truly I tell you, whatever you did for one of the least of these brothers and sisters, you did for me" (Matthew 25:40).

Maybe you cheat on that math test you didn't study for because, hey, you need a good grade, and maybe you get away with it, but for some reason, when you pray, it feels like your prayers are bouncing off the ceiling. You're feeling what the Bible calls conviction. Your sin is literally separating you from a relationship with the God who made you. "But your iniquities are separating you from your God, and your sins have hidden his face from you so that he does not listen" (Isaiah 59:2).

And once Satan has gotten you to that point one time, he will take you back to that horrible moment as many times as he can. We've all been there, but we don't have to stay there.

The Opinions of the Hotties

Being a teenager is a unique moment in life. It's a time when people are good at observing the world but don't have much experience living in it yet. It's easy to see life but hard to know what it means. It's easy to identify hotties but difficult to know how to feel about them.

It's so crazy to me that I can think through the hotties on my list from 1999 and still remember how important their opinions were to me. They were boys who lived with their parents and played video games, and now that I look at them from this place of more maturity, I can smile and say to my former self, "Oh, little Scarlet! Don't worry about these boys! You've got your whole life ahead of you!"

I suspect that your future self might look back at the things you spend all your time thinking about today and say, "Oh, younger self, don't worry about what that guy said. Don't worry about how you had corn stuck in your teeth at the exact moment the tallest linebacker on the team finally struck up a conversation with you. You've got your whole life ahead of you."

What the hotties think doesn't matter for very long. The opinions of hotties and all the other people in all other places are fickle and fleeting and often look foolish when we are looking back. And rarely are they worthy of prime mattress-hiding placement.

But there is one opinion that matters. There is one first opinion that was shared with the first girl and her first boy. And even though they sinned and we sinned, that first opinion can still be heard because the work of Jesus makes it so.

"Then God said, 'Let us make man in our image, according to our likeness.' . . . And it was so. God saw all that he had made, and it was very good indeed" (Genesis 1:26, 30–31).

For the Goody-Goody and the Train Wreck (Hint: You Are Probably Both)

So maybe you don't cheat on tests. Maybe you spend a lot of brainpower feeling angry and superior over people who do. I don't know whether you're the girl who tries to keep all the rules or whether you're the girl who has broken them and doesn't know how she's going to stop and put her life back together. I'll tell you this though: I've been both, and both girls need the same thing. Girls who have messed up and girls who have exhausted themselves trying not to, girls who break rules and girls who bow to them, girls who try and fail and girls who fail to try, all need Romans 5.

Romans 5:15–17 tells us that sin came into the world through one person, and it tells us that one other person, Jesus, took on the punishment for the sins of all who would believe in Him and offered them new life.

We all need to know that even though the first boy and the first girl broke God's rule and broke our hearts and bought the lies and ruined God's original plan, Jesus fixed everything for us. He obeyed for us, believed for us, lived for us, died for us, and rose for us, so that in Him, God can say again, "It is very good indeed." Neither kind of girl, the goody-goody or the train wreck, can do anything good enough to make God love her more or anything bad enough to make God love her less. Jesus kills the lies and restores the opinion and makes us valuable forever.

This reality I'm talking about—that we are loved and forgiven and approved and free because of what Jesus did for us—is what Christians often call "the gospel." The word *gospel* means "good news." When we look at the gospel, this message that Jesus came to deliver, we see that His love for us is the only true, forever, trustworthy love we can count on.

Hotties will let us down. Every last one of them, no matter the degree of hotness.

But we're not living to impress hotties—as much as it feels like we might be. We're not even living to impress God Himself; He's already and eternally impressed.

You won't look perfect and act perfect. You won't string enough days in a row where you haven't done something you're ashamed of. If there were a set number of "good" days that could make you holy or if you were even capable of that, Jesus' death would have been the *most pointless thing ever*.

Hotties will let us down. Every last one of them. no matter the degree of hotness.

When I look to my past and remember seventh grade, when I was unloved and humiliated by a boy with spiky hair and a slightly cooler status than mine, I'm not looking far enough. When I look back farther and remember the cross, it's then that I remember the biggest truth and the truest love. The ultimate act of love was when Jesus allowed Himself to be cut off from the perfect love of His Father and He suffered the greatest humiliation so you and I could be free and whole and safe.

The older you get, the more times you'll mess up, and the more times you mess up, the clearer you'll see the weight of this magic love and what it means for your life.

Get this—if your happiness rests on Jesus' ability to love you, you will never be let down, and through the cross, you will always know where to look to remember that you are loved and beautiful and enough.

A Way Better List

I no longer keep a hottie list, but I still frequently misplace my identity. I've found, as an adult, that one of Satan's best strategies is to make me feel that the approval of someone on a fancy list will make me happy and give my soul peace.

I can still find myself living in the past and living for lists, even though my name has already made it onto the only list that matters (see Revelation 13:8 for more on this one).

Maybe for you, it's middle school hotties or the linebacker on the varsity football team (I liked that guy too). Or maybe you're trying to get on the president's honor roll list. Maybe you're trying to get Harvard's attention by being on the list of students with the highest SAT scores. *Side note: There was a guy in my graduating class who got a PERFECT score, and yes, he graduated from Harvard. I keep tabs.*

Or maybe you *don't* want to be on a list. Maybe it seems like your name is permanently engraved onto a less-than-lovely list, and you wish there were some kind of powerful eraser that could make it go away.

Maybe you've been involved in one too many decisions that have made all your classmates move your name to the "do not invite" list.

Whatever the lists are, we're all looking at them. We all want our names on this one and off that one.

For me, when I'm walking in weakness, the lists I linger on are almost identical to the lists I looked to as a teenager. They are still all about who is paying attention to me and what I'm accomplishing. Who likes me? Who can label me "approved"?

If I get on a best seller list, will people I admire consider me successful?

If so-and-so retweets that thing I said about ice cream sandwiches that I thought was so clever, does that mean I've "arrived"?

If I wear the jeans that fray at the ankle, get the right kind of hair scrunchie, get in shape, have better hair, and so on, will people I do life with think I'm on the cool list?

I'm thirty-two! When this book comes out, I'll be THIRTY-THREE. And I still catch myself longing to be on lofty lists.

And it's embarrassing. And it's sad. And it's wrong.

Sometimes, I realize I'm living for lists—best seller lists, Twitter lists, cool-people lists—and I feel shame. I feel like my dad just discovered my hidden hotties.

And that's actually pretty accurate.

Because God loves us, the Holy Spirit is always making us aware of hidden motives and idols and things that feel right but will wreck our lives.

Our heavenly Dad pulls "hottie lists" out from underneath the mattresses because He loves us and wants us to find worth in Him alone.

But Satan is so quick to twist the words of God, just as he did with the first girl in the garden. He twists God-given conviction into shame and makes us feel like our hottie lists are being discovered over and over and over by everyone.

He'll even twist Scripture in a way that condemns.

"Well done, good and faithful servant." You? Are you kidding me right now?

"Those he justified, he also glorified." So how many Instagram stories have you wasted your time on today?

He'll even twist moments of growth and sanctification. He whispers, *Look how bad you are/were/will be. You'll never be holy. You'll never make the cut. You'll never be on anyone's good list. Whose bad list are you on right now?*

Here's the awesome thing. No matter how much shame I feel about the original hottie list and every list I've idolized since, Jesus has already put my name on the holy list in the book of life.

Romans 5:5 says that hope doesn't put us to shame because God's love has been poured into our hearts.

My shame is Jesus' shame, and Jesus' shame was nailed to a cross. Jesus' holiness is my holiness, and my "holiness" can never add anything.

So, how come we still live like our hottie lists are being found?

Because, we are forgetful.

The accuser may say that Luke 19:17 ("Well done, good servant!") isn't for you. But that's a lie. It is for you because when you become a follower of Jesus, you are, once and for all, no longer you, but Christ in you (Galatians 2:20).

You won't get a "well done" because of any list you've made or any list you're on or any secret you've hidden or any person you've impressed. You'll get a "well done" because Jesus has done well.

Living with the knowledge that you can be guilt-free today and guilt-free forever can give you the freedom to smile and walk humbly, brushing off hottie-related hurts, and realizing that you are already walking in the only identity that really matters. You are a girl who Jesus loves. "Ayyyeeeeeee!"

Chapter 2

THE FANNY-PACK FAIL

The first time I noticed I wasn't trendy at all was during a choir class. All it took was for me to look around and notice that all the girls had jeans that were fitted at the hips and flared at the bottom.

My jeans? Wrong in every way. They scrunched where they should have flared. They sagged where they should have clung. They were high waisted when everything was low rise. They were the opposite of flattering. Like many of my early fashion decisions, they were wrong in all the ways something could be wrong.

See, back when lockers and PE uniforms were part of my life, I developed a little habit of purchasing the trends exactly one to two seconds after the trend stopped being trendy.

It's kind of impressive how good I was at terrible trend timing. I won't bore you with the entire list of things I was too late on (just a few . . . Abercrombie jeans, Pogs, eyelid glitter, butterfly hairclips, boyfriends). But here is kind of how it would go for me. I'll use crossbody fanny packs as an example (you probably have no idea what those are, but bear with me; replace "crossbody fanny pack" with anything cool, and the same process applies).

- Step One: Notice that all the cool girls in my class are wearing plastic, brightly colored fanny packs, but not around their waists. Rather, they are wearing the fanny packs slung over one shoulder, like a crossbody bag.
- Step Two: Notice that all the cool girls in my class are still doing this, months later, while I am still definitely not doing this.
- Step Three: Spend a few weeks studiously researching fanny packs and thinking about whether I needed one from Claire's or from the Icing.
- Step Four: Realize that Macy's also sells plastic fanny packs now. Fanny packs as crossbody bags are, without a doubt, all the rage. This is a complicating factor.
- Step Five: Think about how to ask my parents to buy me a hot pink, completely plastic fanny pack from Macy's, even though it's not a holiday and there is no real reason for me to ask.

- Step Six: Remember that my mom is out of town, so maybe I should wait to ask her until she gets back.
- Step Seven: Present my parents with a two-page Christmas list with PINK PLASTIC FANNY PACK FROM MACY'S highlighted and starred and underlined in every color.
- Step Eight: Accept that Christmas is still two and a half months away and I'll have to wait.
- Step Nine: Feel every wrapped present around the Christmas tree on Christmas Eve, trying to figure out where the fanny pack might be.
- Step Ten: Open the much-anticipated gift.
- Step Eleven: Hear my mom say, "Scarlet, the pink plastic ones looked so CHEAP! I got you BLACK LEATHER because it's classy and it will last forever."
- Step Twelve: Hide my deep, despondent disappointment over the color and material of the fanny pack.
- Step Thirteen: Spend hours staring at my reflection in the mirror, with the fanny pack draped over my body anyway.
- Step Fourteen: Count the seconds until school resumes in January, so I can walk

through those cafeteria doors FINALLY being cool.

- Step Fifteen: Enter the building. **No one wears fanny packs anymore.**
- Step Sixteen: Out of a sense of duty, because my mother spent money on this very black, 100 percent nonplastic fanny pack, endure the entire second half of the school year being the only girl who wears fanny packs anymore and the only girl in the history of school to wear one made out of a grown man's material.

So, that was obviously a long time ago. The crossbody fanny pack's moment has passed, and since that snippet of time in my life, truly everything about me has changed (except my eyebrows; they still, for some reason, grow straight up/vertical instead of normal/sideways like they're supposed to), but despite maturity and life change and all that, it is STILL so easy for me to look back at who I was and how I felt walking through those cafeteria doors and feel like that is my identity NOW. I still sometimes feel like the only girl in school with a leather fanny pack.

Doesn't that sound crazy? That a fully grown, married mother with a job and good health and countless wonderful life things can still sometimes feel like an awkward and unloved and off-trend teenager?

And I don't know how you can do it today, with Instagram being a thing you deal with. I know how hard it is for me—well past the stage you'd assume people still care about what's cool and what's not—to see women who look more put together who are wearing things and eating things and going places I'm not cool enough to know about.

It's really easy to look out at *them*, your peers, and make a long list of what they have that you don't. But get this: even if your mind has been 100 million percent fixated on what you look like and what you have and who you are meant to be in this world, who you were does not define you.

What you once had or didn't have does not define you. What you once did or didn't do does not define you.

Being the one-second-too-late, one-color-too-wrong fanny-pack wearer twenty years ago doesn't have anything to do with who I am now.

Let me say it this way:

> "Do not be afraid, for you will not be put to shame; don't be humiliated, for you will not be disgraced. For you will forget the shame of your youth. . . . Indeed, your husband is your Maker—his name is the LORD of Armies—and the Holy One of Israel is your Redeemer; he is called the God of the whole earth." (Isaiah 54:4–5)

You may not be in the same situation as the girls who first read these verses, but the same grace is for you. God is the coverer of your shame.

The lie you told, the promise you broke, the test you cheated on, the boy you didn't date, or the thing you didn't own— none of that defines you. And none of that shame you sometimes feel can withstand the loving gaze of your good Father.

Maybe you were that girl. Liar. Failure. Disappointment. But Jesus says those aren't your names, because you are His, and His death reclaims your past in full. The gospel redefines who you were.

The lie you told, the promise you broke, the test you cheated on, the boy you didn't date, or the thing you didn't own—none of that defines you. And none of that shame you sometimes feel can withstand the loving gaze of your good Father.

A Photo Shoot with NO FANNY PACKS

When I was a young teen, I went to a "Glamour Shots" birthday party. There was a place at the mall, somewhere near Burbank, where you could get "professional" photos taken. There were big lights and long lenses and silver reflector square thingies and watercolor backdrops, and it was so extremely grown-up.

My mother saved my glamour shots and gave them to me a few years ago. In the one I'm mentioning here, I wore a classic, white, faux-fur halo and what basically looked like a Tickle Me Elmo suit. I remember I felt very snazzy in my borrowed, full-body feathers.

So, until last year, that was my one experience with headshots. And that means, until last year, 100 percent of my headshots featured feathers, proudly and exclusively.

So, when Mary, the wonderful lady who does marketing at the publishing company I work with, emailed me, asking for a headshot to put into a catalog, I panicked. *All I have is a glamour shot from 1999, and I'm pretty sure I don't have my fuzz blouse and fluff crown anymore!* But I did some cyber research of local photographers and found one on Instagram. She said yes. We took pictures. No fuzzy clothes were involved.

So now I've had two headshot experiences. And really, taking teen glamour shots and adult author photos felt similar. On both occasions, I stared into a large lens, wondering what to do with my hands and face, hoping to look normal and poised. On both occasions, I frantically wondered if my Adam's apple was showing. (It was. It always does. I don't know why. We'll delve more into the topic of my female Adam's apple in chapter 4.) On both occasions, I finished the session and waited and wondered if my face would look better than real life or far, far worse. On both occasions, I spent a larger-than-normal chunk of time before and after expending an exorbitant amount of brainpower thinking about what I look like.

Maybe you're like me sometimes. Like when you're at a Glamour Shots birthday party, wearing a red feather boa in Burbank, or when you're trying to smile naturally for the photo that's going in the yearbook, or when you're sitting under the overhang outside of the gym, waiting for your ride home from school, and you're glaring at the impossibly perfect cheerleader who is wearing the exact perfect thing in the exact perfect size and making it look so easy, and you get really caught up in "looking the part," whatever that part may be.

We all go through high school. We all have to be photographed for things (school pictures, family Christmas photos, etc.). We all want to be beautiful.

But "looking the part," whatever part you are after, being "on trend," regardless of the trends that matter to you, is so HARD. It's also so shallow. It's such an easy, empty thing to get caught up in, and still I get caught up in it all the time. Am I doing the wrong thing with my hands again? Are furry halo hats making a comeback? Why are you doing this to me, Adam's apple?

I want my life to be about helping others see the most beautiful thing in the world—the hope and peace of living for Jesus Christ.

You know what I wish I'd wonder instead?

How can my kindness point my friends to Jesus?
How can my actions point my neighbors to Jesus?

I want my life to be about helping others see the most beautiful thing in the world —the hope and peace of living for Jesus Christ.

That's it. And there are no glamour shots for that. But there is a Holy Spirit and a special word for hearts that long for beauty.

"Set your minds on things above . . ."

- — Jesus
- — grace
- — the love of God
- — the smile of God
- — Jesus
- — Jesus
- — Jesus

". . . not on earthly things . . ."

- — name-brand clothes
- — friend goals
- — Instagram followers
- — academic achievements
- — dating wins
- — good hair days

". . . For you died, and your life is hidden with Christ in God. When Christ, who is your life, appears, then you also will appear with him in glory" (Colossians 3:2–4).

You don't have to be so concerned with "looking the part," even if you were 100 percent wrapped up in it all of two pages ago. God knows all and loves you anyway. Your past is forgiven. Your glory is sure. And when you focus on Jesus, I think you'll know what to do with your hands.

From Fanny Packs to Freedom

Finding my way from fanny-pack bondage to freedom is, honestly, something that is still happening. I used to hear older Christians say things like that about any number of struggles, and I'd be disappointed. I'd think, *Surely if you try hard enough, strive strictly enough, be holy enough, you can eventually be awesome.*

It's easy to believe that.

I just wish I'd realized sooner that it's impossible to be good enough to feel good enough.

I wish I'd realized sooner that the truest and most free-ing thing on planet Earth is the fact that, as it says in Isaiah 64:6, our very best efforts are "like filthy rags" (NIV). And even though that's true, we won't be put to shame, as it says in Isaiah 54:4.

Knowing that and believing it, we can throw in the towel in our fight for approval. We already have it. It means we get to rest in Jesus' perfection and accept His forgiveness for our failures. It means we get to watch as His grace, through that truth, slowly but surely makes us more like Him.

A Winnie-the-Pooh Backpack

I don't think the fanny-pack fail painted a complete enough picture for you. So, let's talk about more things I didn't get quite right. First, you need to know that the wearer of the backpack I coveted with a deep covetousness (what was it with me and bags?) was a girl who ended up being one of my best friends.

But a few years earlier, we were on different planets.

Liz had friends. Liz had perfect skin. Liz had a Winnie-the-Pooh backpack. I know that doesn't *sound* cool for teenagers, but just trust me: it was.

I think what was *actually* cool about Liz was the confidence she wore, but as my young mind tried to decipher what it was that made people want to hang with Liz and laugh with Liz and invite Liz to parties, I just assumed it was the backpack.

Let me describe it to you.

It was a stuffed Winnie-the-Pooh with shoulder straps. But it was floppy. It hung loose, casual and cool. And it was facing outward. It had a zipper, so you could put things in it. It was, essentially, a purse that was also simultaneously a stuffed animal.

I needed it. (I think I might still want one.)

It was my ticket to popularity. I was sure of it.

As seemed to be the trend of my life, my mom did buy me what I asked for, but a version that was just *a little bit* wrong.

I'll start with the overall posture of the Winnie-the-Pooh. It was too stiff. I mean, it might as well have been an actual stuffed animal, rather than a purse that was sort of a stuffed animal. Basically, my Pooh looked as uptight and panicked as I felt inside on a daily basis. Liz's Pooh was easy breezy.

Also, while Liz's cool Pooh hung off her back facing outward, so you could see Pooh from the front if you were walking behind her, my Pooh clung to my back. Desperate. Needy. Begging you not to discover its hidden hottie list.

Whatever it was, once again, much like the fanny-pack fiasco, I was ashamed of it. Yet I wore it because my mom had bought it for me and because I guess part of me thought, "Better to have the wrong Pooh than no Pooh at all."

Although I can't say that I have the life experience of owning the perfect Winnie-the-Pooh backpack, I can say with certainty that even if I'd had that backpack, my quest for fulfillment by way of backpack was misguided. The Pooh would have disappointed.

I'm guessing that if you're reading this, that thing you really want has nothing to do with Winnie-the-Pooh. But if you just replace "Winnie-the-Pooh" with Adidas or Free People or Forever 21, I think you know what I'm talking about.

We see people around us who seem to have it together, and we want what they have. It's a part of the human experience. And you can either spend your entire life chasing things that will not satisfy you or make you happy for longer than half a second, or you can learn to rest in the right things.

Focusing on the Right Thing

This morning, I spent time with Jesus. This doesn't always happen the way I'd like it to. In my mind, the perfect time with Jesus would involve fuzzy socks, hot black coffee in my YETI Lowball, and some form of biscotti. There would be perfect, peaceful silence. The temperature in the room would be ideal, and as I touched the Good Book, it would fall open to the most perfect verse that would both convict and encourage me. And I would talk to Jesus until our conversation was over, my heart was full, and I was ready to live another day.

And you can either spend your entire life chasing things that will not satisfy you or make you happy for longer than half a second, or you can learn to rest in the right things.

In reality, I wake up to the sound of my three-year-old screaming that her five-year-old sister took her blue tights with holes in them. If I do manage to escape the screaming, I still hear it faintly from the other room. I make my coffee, but my YETI is dirty because I forgot to hit the On button on the dishwasher, so I have to use the mug that lets the heat out. Sometimes, God's Word convicts me and breaks my heart over my sin. Other times, I feel more like I'm alone than like I'm spending time with the Creator of the universe. Like any relationship, there are times things are clicking and times when they aren't.

But that's not because Jesus is distant. Jesus never changes. "Jesus Christ is the same yesterday, today, and forever" (Hebrews 13:8).

It's because I get distant. It's because I change. It's because I run to and from pursuits for comfort and happiness that will never comfort me or make me happy.

Although I never got the right Pooh, I did end up dating the guy I wanted to date. That ended in a breakup. I got the grades I thought I should get, but that didn't lead to a perfect life and future. I even wound up with the job I always dreamed of doing since I was younger than you are—writing books like this one! I love it so much. But I still get hurt feelings. I still fail. I still stub my toe on the stool in my kitchen. I still worry about friendships. I still question my value. I can still spend half a day trapped in my room because there's a spider in the hall. I can still feel hurt over the fanny packs and Pooh bags from my childhood.

No "good thing" can make our lives meaningful or satisfying. Jesus is the *only* thing. He knows it. He so wants us to know it that it killed Him.

I once heard a pastor named Matt Chandler talking about how so many Christians view the afterlife as "ghosty," and I loved that he used that word. He was explaining that when God remakes heaven and earth, we will have actual physical (perfect) bodies. Not ghosty ones.

When I was a teenager, one of the reasons I had a hard time connecting with God was because I had a "ghosty" view of Him. I didn't view Him as someone who would talk back to me. I didn't think He could really touch my life or heal me of an eating disorder (more on that in the next chapter). I didn't see Him as a living being that could bring His Word to my mind right in the moment I needed it. I didn't realize that His Word could come alive in me and change me. I didn't think it could help me to stop worrying and pining and striving and crying all the time.

But He can and He is and it did.

And He is still solid and speaking, and His Word is still working.

And because I have learned and am still learning to focus on the right things, to view my current self as the person Jesus made me to be, I can giggle at my past Pooh problems. And I can even cry with gratitude, because although it's silly to me now, it wasn't then. Although I have freedom now, I didn't then.

But because of who Jesus is, I'm not who I once was.

I used to think pink plastic fanny packs and droopy, not-stiff Winnie-the-Pooh bags were it. I used to think I needed the cutest, coolest, sweetest, strongest guy in my class to be in love with me.

I used to look back at who I was—the choices I made, the people I let down, the wrong things I did—and it would make me actually cringe. But over the past few years, I've learned that I can look at my past differently.

Because of Jesus, because He left His throne in heaven and humbled Himself for me and kept the Law perfectly for me and died sacrificially for me and broke death triumphantly for me, nothing else can shame me. I can remember even my past cringe-worthy moments with gratitude.

WOW, look at how desperate and broken I was. And Jesus still did all that for me. I must be really loved.

From fanny packs to freedom. From death to life. From hopelessness to finding out you don't need a new string of second chances because Jesus died so you could live with constant and forever hope.

The gospel does that.

The gospel moves our focus off of ourselves and our failures and onto our Savior and our future as His daughters.

It's an amazing thing. It really is. And it's not just for when you're old and gray. It's something you can believe and live today.

You don't have to look the part or strive to define yourself as cool or trendy or godly. Jesus has defined you.

"If anyone is in Christ, [s]he is a new creation; the old has passed away, and see, the new has come!" —2 Corinthians 5:17

Chapter 3

BREAD SMOOSHING MY GRANDMA

When I was younger, I had an idea so brilliant that it had to be executed immediately. I knew what needed to be done, and I went for it.

I sprinted to the kitchen, opened the pantry, removed two slices of bread, and then, with bread in hand, I marched into the living room and smooshed the now palm-warmed slices right into my lovely grandmother's face. I made sure to keep the increasingly damp bread on her face for several seconds and rub it around a little, because of course I did. Then I walked away.

My grandma isn't the type of person who should ever receive this type of treatment, not that there's a type of person who *should*. But my grandma is a noticeably classy lady. Her put-togetherness is well above average. *Regal* is a word that comes to mind. She's poised. She's kind. She's calm. Her clothes are wrinkle-free and timeless, while somehow also being trendy and age appropriate. She's kind of like the unicorn of grandmothers, and she didn't deserve a face full of skin-wettened wheat bread. And yet there she sat, aghast and crumb coated.

That was the one and only time I ever saw my grandma upset. She stood up, wiped the bread bits out of her eyes, and said something like, "Scarlet . . . you don't do that! You don't put bread in a person's face!"

Even then, I remember thinking, *Of course. That was a very bizarre thing to do to a person, and why bread, and why her?* Truth be told, I just really wanted to do it.

Also, I thought of the worst dad joke ever, and I KNOW, okay? But I thought of it, so now I'm writing it out.

I was caught bread-handed.

Anyway, thank goodness I'm not defined by that one moment in time. Could you imagine? What if that one stupid, weird, crumbly, smoosh-centric decision was my defining life moment? What if my sweet grandma only ever thought of me as the bread-handed face smoosher?

Thankfully, I never repeated that experience, but I have often found myself making choices that were dumb or painful or even dangerous. Over and over again, I've caught myself with bread in hand, wondering what just happened and how I could be so wrong. Some of my unwise urges have been silly and strange, like bread smooshing my grandmother. Others were serious and destructive, like the bad diet that almost killed me.

Way Beyond Bread Smooshing

In high school, I had a fairly normal body image. I didn't *love* what I looked like, but I was okay with myself. I wasn't skinny. I wasn't fat. And I didn't think about it all that often. I ate when I was hungry. I found a way to work in two packs of Sour Patch Straws every day between classes, and I didn't have a complex about it. Sometimes, my clothes would get tight, and I'd try to eat less Sour Patches and more vegetables and run a few extra laps after cheerleading practice.

Normal. Healthy. Maybe a little too much candy, but totally okay.

Then I graduated. I met more people. I met more skinny people. I met more opinionated people. I had more control over my life. I wasn't eating every meal at my parents' house anymore. I was able to make my own choices, and one day, I noticed that my clothes were a little tight. My clothes were tight, and my brain told me to be prettier, and cutting candy wasn't enough.

So, I went on a diet.

And then my diet got stricter.

And then stricter.

And then it was crazy strict.

At first I lost weight quickly by eating really healthy, like meat-and-vegetables-only healthy.

And eating healthy is GOOD, which is why I thought I was okay. But "healthy and okay" quickly became very unhealthy and *very* not okay.

I became obsessed. Obsessed with calories. Obsessed with serving sizes. Obsessed with what size my jeans were. Obsessed with MYSELF.

Not normal. Not healthy. Totally not okay.

The people closest told me they were concerned. Why was I so skinny? Why did I refuse to eat after 5:00 p.m.? Did I know there were foods other than zucchini in the world? Why had I lost so much weight so quickly?

And I would jump to my own defense.

"I'm fine, everyone! I'm healthy! Meat and vegetables are good for you! I'm eating things God created!"

The problem was, I wasn't eating them to be healthy. I was eating them to be skinnier. And skinnier. I was eating them to feel pretty, and to feel in control. And I wasn't eating them often enough. And it was only getting worse.

When I Knew It Was Bad

One day, I was eating dried fruit at the airport. It was the first time I'd been on an airplane alone, maybe the first time I'd ever felt truly by myself. I had some cash in my wallet and I bought a magazine, just because I could.

I felt so adult.

In between articles on shampoo and haircuts for your face shape (I still don't know how to determine what face shape I have), I would count the number of raisins and dried pineapples I was eating because, as any "healthy" person knows, it's all about "calories in, calories out." If you eat fewer calories than you burn in a day, you'll lose weight. But, I mean, I was actually counting raisins. Not donut holes, raisins.

Raisin counting was way beyond bread smooshing, but I wasn't at rock bottom yet. Getting there.

You see, if you're wanting to lose weight in a healthy way, exercising and eating good-for-you foods is a great thing to do. But like many great things, when you get so wrapped up in yourself, a good thing can become a destructive thing that can absolutely ruin your life.

But like many great things, when you get so wrapped up in yourself, a good thing can become a destructive thing that can absolutely ruin your life.

The dried fruit was great. The fixation with counting raisins wasn't. So, I was flipping through my magazine, thinking I was okay, but somewhere along the way, I lost count. I lost count of the raisins and the dried banana chips, and I realized that I wasn't sure if I was under my calorie goal for the day.

Was it ten raisins or fifteen? How many pounds are in five raisins? Oh no! The banana chips have more calories for sure. HOW MANY BANANA CHIPS HAVE I EATEN RIGHT NOW?

I was clearly and dangerously past a healthy eating phase. I was consumed with calories. Consumed with weight. The pressure I was placing on myself to look and feel the right way was completely crushing me. And now I'd lost count of my dried fruit.

So, looking around and realizing no one knew me, I got up, found the public bathroom, and made myself throw up. I didn't even really hesitate. My idol of "health" was demanding my full devotion. Failure was not an option, so I took matters into my own hands and threw up.

Here's what I felt:

- ✔ instant shame
- ✔ extreme self-hatred
- ✔ complete despair
- ✔ confusion
- ✔ fear
- ✔ almost-immediate depression

I was disgusted with myself. *How did this happen? Does that make me a bulimic now?*

That could have been the moment that broke my obsession. I can't tell you how much I wish my eyes had been fully opened to my brokenness in that airport bathroom. I wish so much the miscounted raisin ordeal had been my one and only bulimic moment. But that day just moved me farther down the dark road I was already running.

Not only had I done something dysfunctional and self-centered and just plain gross, but throwing up didn't actually make me skinny. It makes you *gain* weight; it messes with your metabolism.

Listen to me: it's terrible. It starts a deadly cycle. It makes your body think that you're starving, so your body will hold on to every calorie, unsure if it will be able to get more in the future. That makes you look less like you want to look and live less like you want to live and feel less like you want to feel. All while hurting you.

I found myself doing it more and more often because I was always so hungry but didn't want to feel full. I felt horrible and sick all the time.

But I kept doing it.

I believed lies.

I believed eating would make me ugly, and I believed that feeling empty would make me skinny.

I believed that skinny meant I'd be beautiful, and being beautiful meant I'd be approved.

I wanted to be loved and admired and approved. And I was literally destroying myself to get there.

The anxiety of living like this is insane. A secret like this darkens every moment, so your life becomes almost unrecognizable.

Living with sin makes you paranoid.

I know it because I've lived it, but the Bible tells us that too: "The wicked flee when no one is pursuing them" (Proverbs 28:1).

You know the feeling. *Everybody knoooooows.* Maybe you don't even see your sin as "wicked." That's

The anxiety of living like this is insane. A secret like this darkens every moment, so your life becomes almost unrecognizable.

because Satan loves to make us have wrong feelings about ourselves and what separates us from God, but we still know to keep secrets. We still know to hide even if no one is trying to find us out.

If you're more of a by-the-book type of girl, Satan will take your sin and put it on a Jumbotron in your mind. He will try to convince you that God will never forgive you. Your parents will disown you. Your friends will be disgusted by you.

All lies. But still we run.

Sin, all sin, is wickedness before a holy God. It is serious, dead serious. BUT if you are a follower of Christ, all that wickedness in your heart and all the secrets you hide are completely erased, forgiven, gone, because Jesus took the punishment you had coming for you. Jesus ran to the cross with no sin. He proved the deathly seriousness of sin by dying, fully and finally, for the things we do, the things we rationalize, and the things we hide.

So crazy.

What I'm trying to say is, either way, sin gives paranoia, and Jesus gives perfection.

Even if you're not a naturally anxious person, you always feel like someone is after you when you are walking a path of sin. You always feel like you're about to get caught. You are shaking off a constant whisper that says, "You're about to be found out, and you're going to lose everything."

The enemy is so convincing at making us believe that if we get caught, our lives will be over. If our sin is exposed, everything is ruined.

God actually says the exact opposite. He says to confess, and you will receive mercy (Proverbs 28:13).

Looking back on all those lies I believed, what brings tears to my eyes is that I was *already* loved. I was already adored by the only One who matters. I was already free, and yet I was living in secret and working myself into a frenzy to gain something I already had. I wanted someone to tell me I was beautiful, and He already had.

God's love for me had nothing to do with a raisin count or a jean size or eyeliner wing precision. His affections had nothing to do with how holy I had or hadn't been the day before, or the hour before, or right as I flushed the toilet and erased the evidence. His love for me had (and has) everything to do with Jesus in my place.

I wanted someone to tell me I was beautiful, and He already had.

His holiness. His good works. His perfection. His beauty. His sacrifice for me. And for you.

Because of Jesus, you are loved.

Because of Jesus, you are approved.

Because of Jesus, your life matters.

Because of Jesus, you have no reason to hide.

But if and when we don't really believe that, we might run elsewhere looking for the feeling we know we should have, the satisfaction we get when someone says, "Good job!" or "You're beautiful!"

We have all that to the max in the pages of God's Word. And any other place we look for it is going to leave us empty and sad and hungry and eventually hating ourselves.

Like so many other destructive things, getting sucked into a sin trap is so difficult because the enemy wants you to believe you're stuck when you're not. And the enemy also loves to downplay the consequences. The truth is, girls die from eating disorders like the one I had. They think they're okay, like I did. They think they'll stop soon. But just like the Bible warns us, all sin leads to death.

Sin leads to death, and death looks hopeless. So, what can we do? Where can we find hope?

Looking for Hope in Books

The first place I looked for answers was at Barnes & Noble. Because, I mean, bookstores smell like fresh paper and new starts, and they are full of wise words about hottie lists and fanny packs.

So, I took my shame to the bookstore, and I pretended I was casually walking past the self-help section of the store. But if someone came up behind me, I hid somewhere else and waited until they walked away.

During one SO CASUAL bookstore outing, I found a few books that were specifically and totally about eating disorders. *Oh wow! This is it!* I just knew it! I was about to be healed and normal and completely okay.

Thank you, bookstore! Thank you for selling wisdom and strange toys no one has ever heard of and Starbucks coffee that you can't use a Starbucks gift card for.

I remember trying to be subtle as I sneakily picked the books up, and I remember wedging the books I found between two unembarrassing books, like *The Catcher in the Rye* and *The Scarlet Pimpernel.* Then I sat in those cushy chairs that are scattered around the store, and I frantically skimmed, looking for something, anything. I wanted to find a fix, a formula.

If someone sauntered by, I raised my secret book up closer to my face to hide the words that would condemn me. Ugly words like *bulimia* and *anorexia* and *kidney failure* and *death.*

My heart raced, and my eyes raced over words as I speed-read every book on the shelf that was remotely about what I was dealing with. But I wasn't finding what I wanted.

I wasn't finding the answer.

I kept finding pages that said things like, "It's a lifelong battle," or "You can do this, but every day for the rest of your life, you'll fight."

I can't remember the names of the books I looked through, but I didn't see a lot of hope for healing. I was killing myself and counting banana chips. I needed hope.

I just wanted to get better. I just wanted it all to be behind me.

Looking for Hope in a Better Book

So, the second place I looked for answers was the Bible. I'd grown up reading it and hearing about it, and I knew what it said about itself, so it seemed worth a shot.

> For the word of God is living and effective and sharper than any double-edged sword, penetrating as far as the separation of soul and spirit, joints and marrow. It is able to judge the thoughts and intentions of the heart. (Hebrews 4:12)

I knew I was supposed to believe all that was true, but I didn't have a whole lot of firsthand experience at that time. I was mostly good at *not* reading the Bible, or at least not reading it for myself.

But looking in the Bible during those dark days, I kept finding my way to one specific verse. It was almost uncanny how often this verse would be what I turned to or what just found its way to me via radio or sermon or conversation. It was kind of like how these days I feel like I'm always passing a Chick-fil-A sign. Once something powerful crosses your path, it is hard to ignore it. The Holy Spirit was getting my attention. He was using His very alive, very interactive Word to pierce me and show me what I needed to do to get unstuck.

My Chick-fil-A verse was Proverbs 28:13: "The one who conceals his sins will not prosper, but whoever confesses and renounces them will find mercy."

Mercy sounded so great. I'd never wanted anything so much, and nothing felt farther away.

God would put that verse in my path and that offer in my heart, and I'd audibly say back to Him, "But I can't. It will ruin my life to confess this. I can get past this without confessing. Please, Lord, give me the strength to do it on my own."

But He didn't give me that strength. He knew I couldn't conquer sin and death with my own willpower. He knew He had already crushed on the cross everything that was crushing me. He also knew I needed to bring my secrets out into the light. But I didn't want to, and there was no healing.

I read the truth of God's Word, but I didn't submit to it. I wanted to hide. I was too wrapped up in my fears. But I can tell you from my own experience that none of those fears were rooted in reality. What made sense in my heart was the opposite of what I needed.

Our hearts say, "Be served." Jesus says, "Serve."

Our hearts say to hide the embarrassing parts of our lives. Jesus says to *expose them* so we can overcome them.

See, that's the big thing I was missing. Confession. I was counting and cowering and crying like crazy. But I wasn't confessing.

Preachers have proclaimed it for ages. Moms and dads have echoed it on and on. You might be sick of hearing it, but it's true. It's true now, and it will still be true when you're my age. And there is healing and hope in this truth: Sin cannot grow in the light.

Everything you keep hidden will grow until it is bigger than you and bigger than your ability to control it. Then it will overpower you and eat you alive. It's not pretty. Sin, whichever one you're fighting—sexual impurity, pride, dishonesty, greed, selfishness—is not a light thing; it leads to death, every time. In my case, eating disorders can result in physical death. But all sin leads to spiritual death if it's not brought before Jesus and forgiven.

Your heart and your head will tell you to hide. And when you do, you seem to become that ugly secret. That thing you do that you hate becomes who you think you are. But guess what? You are not that. You never could be that, really. And Jesus hates the fact that you might think you are what you hate. He fought all the reasons we keep things hidden, and He fought the brokenness that lets all of our monsters grow. And He won. He killed those secrets that scare us to death. And if we just bring them into the light, we see that they aren't flesh, but dust. When we confess, we actually hear the emptiness of our secrets from our own mouths. We hear the fakeness of their promises in our own ears. And we can hear the very hope of Jesus when we speak out our confession.

> Jesus says that although your bad choices of the past might have consequences, they don't get to tell you who you are. Defeated things have to keep their mouths shut.

Jesus says you don't have to be slave to that thing. He says you're not defined by that thing.

Jesus says that although your bad choices of the past might have consequences, they don't get to tell you who you are. Defeated things have to keep their mouths shut.

Only Jesus gets to tell you who you are—because you are His.

He made you. He fought for you. He won.

A Piano Recital I'll Never Get Back

For me, the eating disorder didn't only damage my body; it also caused problems in my most important relationships. You might think what you're doing only affects you, but dangerous secrets will cause hurt to the people you love the most.

My little sister is super talented. She's good at everything she's ever tried. Although I dabbled in all sorts of activities, like cycling and poetry and making completely inedible homemade peanut butter cups, I quit most of said activities as soon as things got a little bit hard, or as soon as I tasted the first bite of my "how can this possibly taste so bad?" handcrafted Reese's wannabe. My sister stuck with things, though, and she got particularly amazing at playing the piano.

Every year, she'd have a recital, and we'd all show up and sit through the millions of piano songs, waiting for my sister's big five minutes in the spotlight.

So, the year I was most intensely stuck in the food dysfunction, I missed her recital. And it wasn't just any recital. It was the most special one of her piano career up to that point. She ended up winning the gold medal. For reference, I have won zero medals for cycling, poems, or peanut butter cups. Not even a participation medal, because I failed to continue participating.

And I just didn't show up to her recital. I remember sitting on the floor of my room, crying. I looked at the clock and knew it was time. I knew that my family had reserved a seat for me. And I couldn't move. I couldn't get up. I couldn't be a person.

I was nineteen at that point, and I just couldn't go sit with a bunch of normal, happyish people at a piano recital. Have you been there? In a skipping-out-on-your-own-life season? If you haven't yet, you might be someday.

I put my fingers on my neck to feel my pulse. That's something I did frequently. I'd get my fingers in the right place and find my pulse. And I'd count. Because I knew that I couldn't keep abusing my body. I knew it was catching up with me. I knew that my organs would fail me at some point, and so I'd obsessively check my pulse. To make sure it was still there. To make sure I was still there. To assess the damage. To see if it was too late.

I tell you about the recital to tell you that sin has sad consequences.

I lived through my eating disorder. I have recovered and gone on to have children. My relationship with my sister is even restored.

But I still feel sorrow at that memory and many others. I still feel deep sadness when I think about skipping out on the people I love. It might not sound like much to you, but while my sister was having a major life moment, I was choosing death over life. Darkness over light. I was choosing me over her. Selfishness over love.

Being Pretty Wasn't Enough

I spent years hoping to be defined by beauty. I wanted to be "the skinny person." I wanted to be the "prettiest one in the room." I really thought that being skinny would equal being pretty, being pretty would equal being peaceful, and being peaceful would equal being happy. But you know what? I sort of achieved my stupid goal. I got skinny. Really skinny. Dangerously skinny. And it didn't make me feel peaceful. It didn't make me feel happy. It made me skip my life and check my pulse. It made me feel uglier than when I wore pants two sizes bigger.

Being skinny and feeling like I'd reached my beauty goal completely let me down. Feeling so trapped AND so wrong was crushing.

The terror I felt over being found out, the way my body ached, and the fact that my actions were hurting the people who loved me—all of it swirled together and was ruining my life. I really had no future hopes or dreams or ambitions. All I felt, all the time, was fear and panic and hopelessness.

But Jesus Healed Me

It was September 10, and I was sitting outside of a Starbucks, with an espresso because I felt so weak, and I just knew I was going to die.

My sin, my secret, was going to kill me.

So, reluctantly, after three and a half years of proving I wasn't strong enough, I obeyed Proverbs 28:13. I sat in my car and made a phone call.

I confessed to my closest person. I said, "I'm going to die. What I'm doing is killing me. I have to tell you a lot of things right now . . ." I was urged to go see a Christian counselor the next day. And I did.

That verse never made complete sense to me until I found myself writing my name on a form in the waiting room of an office with a white noise machine and candles and green throw pillows.

Scarlet Hiltibidal

Reason for visit: Bulimic

Date: September 11, 2008

Just the act of writing it out was devastating to me. I sat in the session and I shared everything. And my sweet counselor surprised me by not being surprised. When you're hiding a shameful secret, you always think people will be surprised if they know it. They rarely are.

She gave me a journal to keep, to write down the things I would experience and what I would eat before I made myself throw up. Because it was something I was doing daily, she assumed I'd have a full journal to share with her at our session the following week.

But I never wrote anything in the journal, because it never happened again.

I left her office, full of shame, with this little paper journal in my shaking hands. They were always shaking. But something was changing. My secrets were dying in the light.

If you have something you need to confess, pray about who you should confess to. Your parents, a counselor, or a leader at church are probably good options. If you want to find freedom, who you tell matters. The people you let into your struggle should be people who will help you walk toward Jesus. Confessing my sin to fellow Christians is what led to my freedom.

After meeting with a counselor, I went to a church service that night. I felt so exposed as I walked in and sat in the balcony. I didn't know the people who were sifting into the rows around me, but I felt like they knew how disgusting I felt. They didn't. But the God who did know called me His beloved.

And then, I went home. And I'm not sure exactly when the miracle happened, but it was definitely that same day. Maybe in the lobby. Maybe in the parking lot. Maybe when I sat down in my car. Maybe it happened the moment I confessed. Whenever it was, God healed me that day.

September 11, 2008.

He pursued, He waited, He urged me to obey—"Daughter, confess, and THEN, you will receive mercy.

Stop hiding and there can be healing. Stop fighting and there can be resting."

I can't even really think about it without crying. Jesus gave me a special, supernatural word, *His* Word. He had given it to me so many times. He'd put it before me in so many ways. And I had disobeyed Him for so long. But then I didn't, and the worn-out prayer I'd been praying for years was answered. I found one moment of surrender, and He changed my whole life. He led me to the greatest moment of freedom I've ever known.

I felt it immediately. In my body. In my brain. Every urge to do dysfunctional things with food was gone. I was free.

That's when I started telling people about Jesus. I'd been a Christian for years, but I didn't understand how much I really needed Jesus until I experienced this miracle in my brokenness.

I witnessed to the guy at the CVS on the corner of 168th, and the people next to me at the laundromat on Pinecrest. I asked people in line at the Panera by my dentist's office if they had faith in God and if they would let me tell them what Jesus had just done in my life.

That was TEN years ago.

Listen, young, beautiful friends of mine: some choices you are making right now are as meaningless as bread smooshing your grandmother. But others are not. You might be choosing to abuse your body, to hurt your soul, or to hurt others. To continue to lie or cheat or treat people badly. Some secrets you are hiding can have lifelong consequences and crush your joy.

But Jesus is real.

The grace He offered the world two thousand years ago is also for today. The power He showed in killing death and lighting the darkness still does those things now. It's also for you. In Jesus, no stupid mistake is the end of your world, because once you have chosen Him, He has already declared you pure, forgiven, beautiful, and many other things. Not because of anything you've done right, but because the object of your hope and the One who saves you from your secrets did everything right.

For you are saved by grace through faith, and this is not from yourselves; it is God's gift— not from works, so that no one can boast.
—Ephesians 2:8–9

Section 2

THE GOSPEL SHAPES
WHO YOU ARE

Chapter 4

HOW TO HIDE A FEMALE ADAM'S APPLE FOR TWELVE YEARS

I know how anatomy is supposed to work. Kind of. I had multiple science classes. I think I even won a science award. I remember very little of the important sciency stuff, but I do know that girls typically don't have Adam's apples. I also know that I *have* an Adam's apple.

I'm not sure when I noticed my Adam's apple. I honestly don't remember if it was during one of my staring-at-my-own-face-in-the-mirror sessions (flip back to the introduction for a play-by-play on this behavior) or if a classmate pointed it out. But somewhere around the time I started caring about how I looked, I noticed that I had a very conspicuous, very large, very manly Adam's apple where there should have been just straight neck.

I don't know. Bodies are weird. What I do know is that it's very uncomfortable, as a teenage girl, to break the mold in any single way. In my opinion, though, having a body part associated with men only is really up there. It's a pretty bad way to stand out.

I think I learned that girls and Adam's apples don't go together when I heard some friends talking about it in the cafeteria. I think it went something like, "Dude, I mean, yeah he's kind of feminine looking, but he's got an Adam's apple. See? That's all the proof I need. He's clearly a dude."

I'm not sure if that's a direct quote. I just know I happened to be standing close enough to a group of guys who were looking at some new student who might not have looked guyish enough for them, and the deciding factor for them in regards to this person's gender was, "Does he have an Adam's apple?"

I remember hearing this conversation happening and lowering my head. Why did I have an Adam's apple? What was going on? It's honestly ridiculous how far in the forefront of my mind this was for my entire educational career.

I was so embarrassed about my female Adam's apple that I made it a point to walk around with my chin pointed down at my chest.

The Gonzo Nose Situation

I also had a pointy-nose problem. I mean, I am still living with that situation, but back then, my face hadn't quite grown into it, and I hadn't accepted it yet.

The only person who ever said anything about the tip of my nose pointing deeply downward was my baby sister (she is a full eight years younger than I am). And she only said it because I said it.

"Hey GONZO," she'd say in that way that people who love each other can joke around—at least I hope it was in that way. (If you're unfamiliar with Gonzo, think about the cast of *The Muppets*. He's the blue one with the long nose.) I laughed and am probably the one who started the joke about myself, but when I was with my peers, it was something I was self-conscious about. Especially when I laughed. When I laughed, I thought my nose looked extra pointy, so I would often cover my mouth with my hand while I laughed and ever-so-subtly push the tip of my nose upward in the process. *When the giggles start, raise the hand as though you are attempting to hold the laughter in, and lightly nudge the ever-toppling nose tip up to a more level elevation. Hold it. Hold it. Push up at the end in hopes that the infinitely dangling nose cap will live a little higher than normal for a few precious moments.*

My Adam's apple coverage and pointy-nose-avoidance strategies were exhausting.

Guys, my Adam's apple coverage and pointy-nose-avoidance strategies were exhausting.

My mind could never rest. Nose, neck, nose, neck, hide, hide, hide.

I so badly wanted the parts of myself that I didn't like, that other people might not like, to be hidden, but you can't really run away from what's on your face.

Joy and Her Ear Spaces

One of my three daughters was left for adoption as an infant in China. She was born without any ears.

On one side of her head, there is no ear at all. It's just skin, with a small indentation. But you can't really notice it with her hair hanging down over it. On the other side, there is some skin that looks a little like an earlobe, but it's lower than an earlobe usually is. So, she has no outer ears on either side.

But to our surprise, after we adopted her, we discovered with the help of doctors that her inner ear functions perfectly. So, with a little hearing aid that is strapped to a headband, she can hear! We didn't expect that when we went to China to adopt her. We spent six months learning sign language as a family so we could communicate with her. And it's a good thing we did, because although she can hear (and there are limitations; she can't wear her hearing aid in or near water, and she can't hear well in crowded, noisy places), she can't speak. So signing is the way she tells us everything she tells us. At home, we try to sign and speak at the same time for her.

Because we know her language, and because she has recovered from her early years of neglect in China, life is relatively normal for her at this point. She's healthy and able to communicate well for her age. She's been home a year and a half, and she can hear and understand English! Isn't that crazy?

So, in most ways, as long as someone around her knows sign language, she lives with little to no limitation.

But the fact remains: she's missing a pair of ears.

Most people have ears. In fact, I don't know anyone else who doesn't have any.

I mean, can you imagine? Maybe you can. Maybe you were born with something missing too. Joy will spend her life (if we don't do reconstructive surgery) seeing a world full of ears and then looking in the mirror and noticing that she doesn't have what everyone else has.

She already *knows* that she's missing them now. I know it, because her little brow scrunches up when she watches me put earrings in. She'll sign, "Pretty earrings, Mommy. I have nothing ears." Or her younger sister will say, "MOMMY. JOY DOESN'T HAVE ANY EARS," like it's a news flash, even though we've covered this, like, every day for over a year and a half.

She knows, but it's not something that often interferes with her confidence because she's constantly surrounded by people who love her, who are used to her differences.

When she notices and points out her earlessness, she is met with praise and love. I often say, "You don't have ears. You are special! Look at your beautiful hair and those pretty eyes! You are BEAUTIFUL! SO beautiful!"

So, to her, it's no big deal right now.

But it will be. I know that it's only a matter of years before the way she looks will cause her some worry or pain. If I, someone with all functioning body parts, and even an extra Adam's apple, could be so insecure about the angle in which the tip of my fully functioning nose points, I know that it's got to be extra difficult for people who are born lacking body parts, or born in ways that make them look dramatically different from other people.

My hope is that by the time Joy reaches the age where kids are extra mean and lacking ears is extra obvious, she will be secure enough in her identity as a fearfully and wonderfully made daughter of God to brush off the lie that she is faulty and embrace the truth that she is favored.

I pray that her mind won't be set on how well her ears are hidden by her hair, but rather, that her mind would be set on things above.

Ears or no ears. Adam's apple or not, blonde or brunette or bald, you are loved.

"Set your minds on things above, not on earthly things" (Colossians 3:2). And why? "For you died, and your life is hidden with Christ in God. When Christ, who is your life, appears, then you also will appear with him in glory" (Colossians 3:3–4).

There's nothing you need to hide when your priorities are lined up with the priorities of your Father. Ears or no ears, Adam's apple or not, blonde or brunette or bald, you are loved. There's nothing to hide.

Hidden in Christ

I'm sitting in a Panera right now. I just finished an iced chai and a pumpkin cookie, and I'm in a cozy fall sweater, feeling those happy fall feelings that come when leaves are changing colors and the annoying how-am-I-sweating-by-just-walking-from-my-front-door-to-the-car thing is a distant memory.

I'm sitting here typing with my head tilted up and back because this booth seat is comfy, and my neck and nose are *fully* exposed (!!!). The nose still droops, and the apple hasn't disappeared, yet here I am. Chin up (even if the nose is still down).

And the only reason I'm able to live in such an exposed and unguarded way is because I learned a very important truth: I can't hide my face. I can't hide my neck. I can't even hide my sin. Numbers 32:23 reminds me that my sin will find me out (NIV).

But here, in Colossians 3, is something real that says we are safe. Our lives—the parts we regret, the mistakes we've made—*are* hidden. Everything that truly needs covering in us is hidden in the best way.

"For you died, and your life is hidden in Christ with God" (v. 3).

When you make a decision to follow Jesus, your old, embarrassing, shameful, stained, doomed self dies. Like, it's gone. It's buried. It's covered in dirt. The stone is rolled in front of the door. It's HIDDEN.

The only way the icky stuff in our lives and hearts can be truly hidden is with Christ in God.

It's in the sacrifice of Jesus that we can find confidence. Not in ourselves. We have manly necks and pointy noses and we're racking up failures like it's going to earn us a college scholarship. But Jesus lived our replacement life. He paid our debt. Jesus took all the real, deeply broken parts of us into Himself and onto the cross. He took our weaknesses and failures into the grave. Then He came out bringing with Him only life. He left the worst we had behind. Hidden and gone and defeated forever. So, we can walk around without carrying the baggage of our pasts or the embarrassments of our present. We can trust God to help us find our confidence in who He is rather than in what we look like.

Listen: I know what it's like out there—out there in school world. When I was in it, I'd look at older people and think, *But they can't really understand. Things are different now.*

But here on the other end, I can see that they really aren't. The trends have changed. The way you talk and text has changed a little. But not really. Today, ten years ago, and three hundred years ago, young women were trying and hoping to be beautiful.

I think of my little girl looking in the big mirror in my bedroom and saying, "Mommy, the mirror told me I'm the prettiest girl."

No one has ever told her differently. The mirror tells her she's pretty. Her mommy tells her God loves her. And she has no reason to think any differently. But someone someday in some way will tell her differently.

I used to feel like everything was okay too, but soon, I got old enough to realize that there were other descriptive adjectives people could use to describe my appearance.

I was still watching cartoons when I realized that some people in the world were told they were pretty, while others, like me, were told they were ugly, looked like a boy, looked weird, had man legs, and/or looked like Gonzo from *Muppet Babies*.

And you never know how all the words and all the moments are stacking up against your soul. Gonzo's nose might be a silly example, but by the time I was eighteen, I had so much appearance-related insecurity that I went to great lengths to HIDE.

Hiding from Mean Guys

There was this guy at my school who was really cruel. I don't know much about why or what his homelife was like. I just know that he talked about us girls and our looks in a demeaning, humiliating way. He picked us apart body part by body part, told us what was wrong, and laughed at us. And he did it all the time.

Seriously. Nightmare.

Each day, I would walk the long way around the school to get to the gym so I wouldn't pass him. Why? Because he said my legs were big and ugly.

That hurt me so much. I mean, obviously. I still remember it like it was yesterday.

So, I came up with a solution. I decided to hide.

I would try to time it just right so that when he was walking down the big stairs, past the cafeteria, outside, down the long sidewalk, and up to the overhang (the place we were supposed to be after school), I could cross to the opposite side of the school. I would pass by the science labs, the faculty bathrooms, the admissions office and art rooms, walk by the ice room and the janitor closet, prance past the portable classroom modules, shimmy along the edge of the outdoor basketball courts, and walk up the other side stairs of the overhang. He was still there, of course, but going half a mile out of my way meant I was on the other side. Farther from him. I didn't have to walk past him. I did that every day.

Sometimes, he still said mean things about how I looked. Sometimes, my mom would come pick me up before he had a chance to. But the point is, I put a lot of effort into hiding from him. I just wish I had known then that there was another option.

I could have handled him in a different way that didn't involve sneaking past the janitor closet. I could have hidden from those hurts by setting my eyes on the One who David says is my refuge and my strength:

> God is our refuge and strength, a helper
> who is always found in times of trouble.
> Therefore we will not be afraid, though the

> earth trembles and the mountains topple
> into the depths of the seas, though its water
> roars and foams and the mountains quake
> with its turmoil. (Psalm 46:1–3)

The thing about Jesus is that He came into the world turning things upside down.

He's still doing it today.

The things that should hurt us and wreck our lives are transformed into things that He works together for our good.

> We know that all things work together for
> the good of those who love God, who are
> called according to his purpose. (Romans
> 8:28)

Jesus is constantly hiding the bad and highlighting the good. He does it with our sin. He does it with our weaknesses. He takes ashes and makes beauty (Isaiah 61:3).

What a testimony it would be if we all stopped hiding because of insecurity and rather started enjoying the security we find in Jesus. Our sins are washed away, so we don't have to hide from them or live our lives in hiding. People wouldn't know what to think! Well, actually, they'd probably be drawn to us because confidence draws people in. People like *that mean guy* could be changed by a supernatural love they may have never experienced.

And that's the awesome thing about the confidence that comes from Christ. It doesn't draw people in and cause them to admire you. It draws them in and causes them to find and experience Christ in you. It leads to more healing, heart change, and salvation.

Living Unhidden in the Best Way

So, the worst stuff is hidden. The perfection of Jesus is ours now. And because of that, we can live free. We don't have to worry about hiding our faces or our non-ears or our "ugly" legs or our fat rolls or our past mistakes. In fact, think of it this way: In Christ, your sin isn't just hidden. It's not just an embarrassing thing that could be found if God looked hard enough. It's GONE.

> As far as the east is from the west, so far has he removed our transgressions from us. (Psalm 103:12)

The shame of your past is gone. And if someone (or your own heart) even tries to bring it up and use it to hurt you, you can say with confidence, "I am forgiven. I am loved! Yes, I have many failures under my belt, but Jesus died and rose for those failures."

Isn't that amazing?

We don't have to worry about hiding our faces or our non-ears or our "ugly" legs or our fat rolls or our past mistakes.

Sometimes I fight in my mind; often I'll do it out loud. I'll begin my prayers by reminding myself who God is and what He's really like. What He's already proven Himself willing to do and capable of. After I get a few sentences out, I remember the truth. I remember how desperately I need Him. How much He had to forgive me for. And then I remember that right then, as I'm praying the prayer, the Holy Spirit is talking to God for me on my behalf. When I don't know what to say, He is understanding what my heart wants to say:

> In the same way the Spirit also helps us in our weakness, because we do not know what to pray for as we should, but the Spirit himself intercedes for us with unspoken groanings. (Romans 8:26)

And I remember that God looks at me with delight.

> The LORD your God is among you, a warrior who saves. He will rejoice over you with gladness. He will be quiet in his love. He will delight in you with singing. (Zephaniah 3:17)

And do you know what? Although that verse is in Zephaniah and was written a long time ago, a long way from here, I know that delighting applies to me. God's delighted singing is for me too, because guess how Zephaniah 3 begins? "Woe to the city that is rebellious and defiled, the oppressive city! She has not obeyed; she has not accepted discipline. She has not trusted in the LORD; she has not drawn near to her God" (vv. 1–2).

Do you know who that sounds like? Me.

I am rebellious. I am defiled. Even at my best, I rebel by being proud. Or I do not obey the perfect law perfectly. I don't always trust God. I neglect to draw near. Woe to me—and you.

But how does He feel about us?

Well, eight verses into the chapter, a subject heading in my Bible says, "Final Restoration Promised." Verse 15 says, "The LORD has removed your punishment."

This book of the Bible was written BEFORE Jesus came. But God always had a plan to restore His people to Him.

We don't have to be the girl who says, "If my dad finds out, he will kill me!"

We know that our God knew everything about us and our wickedness before He laid the foundations of the world. And not only did He not kill us; He allowed His own Son to be killed for us. And that Son, Jesus, willingly died in our place. And in so doing, forgave our sin.

Confessing sin doesn't equal punishment when you belong to God. It equals freedom. Being hidden doesn't mean we are penalized when we are hidden in Christ; it means we are protected.

And you may be reading this and thinking, *Okay . . . but what does that have to do with my nose shape or split ends or the pores on my face?*

Everything. Jesus on the cross has everything to do with everything you do.

See, once this clicks, you won't care as much about the split ends.

When eternal life and amazing grace and joy unspeakable are firmly yours, how you look fades into the background.

Believing what Jesus says about your worth is the only remedy for the exhausting cycle of striving for physical perfection.

Upside-Down Confidence for Today

Maybe you think confidence comes with age or money. Maybe if you have enough money to get a professional hair-dye job every month, you'll have it made. Maybe if you get older, the body parts you're insecure about will morph or grow or shrink or even out. If so, congratulations. As for me, I still have an Adam's apple.

Or maybe you're not sure where confidence comes from. You just know you don't have it and you want it. Or maybe you feel like you have it, but it's so fragile that it's one pimple, bad grade, or breakup away from crumbling.

But you can enjoy a kind of confidence that doesn't depend on your complexion or whether you were born with the best body parts.

I could have walked a fully bulbous, completely protruding female Adam's apple around my high school campus and laughed at myself, if I'd just been confident in the right thing:

> Charm is deceptive and beauty is fleeting,
> but a woman who fears the LORD will be
> praised. (Proverbs 31:30)

So just preach to your heart in this moment, my friends. Charm is deceptive. Noses hang low. Beauty is fleeting. Adam's apples are forever. But the Maker of All delights in His girls. And Jesus is more than enough.

I could have walked a fully bulbous, completely protruding female Adam's apple around my high school campus and laughed at myself, if I'd just been confident in the right thing.

Chapter 5

WHEN EVERYONE HATES YOU BY ACCIDENT

Making your whole class hate you isn't something you typically just stumble into. Being 1,000 percent shunned in a school cafeteria is hard to do without building a certain reputation. But I have been so shunned. I have had that reputation. I have known the full and careful refusal of my entire class to acknowledge my entire existence. I have eaten lunchroom pizza alone. And I've actually learned to enjoy those pretty, delicious, rectangular slices, comforted by my belief that I alone was right and just and that the rest of the world would never understand me. Me, my pizza, and my pride were enough. Shun away, entire world.

So, in this chapter, I'll share a cautionary tale. The tale of the time I managed to make my entire class wish they'd never had to share a yearbook page with me.

More specifically, I will share about the time I became the reason two guys who everyone in our grade loved got expelled.

The Birth of a Reputation

By high school, *people knew me.* They'd known me for a while. Even though my family had moved away when I started middle school, that move was only for one year. Then I returned to the same school in Miami that I had gone to before. So, these people remembered my tendencies. They remembered my personality. I had a reputation, and it wasn't necessarily for always being a team player.

It all started back in second grade, really—the forming of my persona. One day our class of twenty had been particularly unruly while writing our names in cursive ten times during seat work. So, we were punished with a dreaded "No Talk Lunch." No Talk Lunch meant we had to sit and eat our brown-paper-sack lunches in our allotted seventeen-minute time slot in COMPLETE SILENCE, after having sat in complete silence all morning. We were supposed to use the additional silent time to reflect on the several more hours of silence that awaited us when we returned to our desks. It was the worst.

So, during our No Talk Lunch, I absolutely and always kept my mouth totally committed to staying closed. I was urgently focused on keeping my teeth clamped shut, only to open for bites of sandwich. But Mario did not keep his mouth shut. Neither did Kristina with a *K*. They just wouldn't honor the No Talk stipulation of the No Talk Lunch. What was I supposed to do? Just sit there in silence while Kristina with a *K* and Mario SPAT AT THE

LAW AND TAINTED THE LUNCH PUNISHMENT
EXPERIENCE FOR THE REST OF US?

In hindsight, yeah, I guess I *was* supposed to just sit in silence. But instead, I started making a list of disobeyers.

Like a real list, on a piece of paper.

I made an actual, physical list of No Talk Lunch talkers. I made sure they saw me carefully writing their names as I was well prepared to do because I had not been talking while writing our names in cursive ten times during seat work. I took my list of offenders to the teacher and probably hoped that Mario and Kristina with a *K* would get thrown into real prison for what they'd done.

But Mario did not keep his mouth shut. Neither did Kristina with a K. They just wouldn't honor the No Talk stipulation of the No Talk Lunch.

Anyway, that's the kind of child I was. It is understandable that the people who grew up with me, who'd had their names put on lists I handed to teachers, would assume that I was out to get them and all the friends they loved.

There were probably a couple more examples of such behaviors that set me up to be shunned. And then a crazy thing happened.

The Locker Note That Ruined High School

School had just gotten out one day, and I opened my locker to find an unexpected note. I unfolded the wrinkly notebook paper and saw handwriting I didn't recognize.

Dear Scarlet . . .

I won't tell you what the rest of the note said, although I vividly remember every word. I'll just say this. It was inappropriate. It was very graphic. And it ended with a physical threat.

And it was signed by a sweet, shy guy who was rumored to have a thing for me.

I didn't know the sweet guy personally. I just knew that he was shy. I had heard he liked me, and he'd even written me a note and stuck it in my locker once before. But *this* note was insane. This note was even scary.

I walked down the stairs to the cafeteria, staring at my note in shock. My dad, who was picking me up that day, met me on the stairs and saw my panicked face.

Sidebar: My dad adopted me when I was eight. He was on the SWAT team, catching bad guys for ten years, before he was promoted to police helicopter pilot. His muscles look like something from a Superman cartoon, and his pinky finger was shot off during a drug bust. My dad is trained. My dad is tough. My dad is THE man.

So, when he saw my eyes while I read the note, he clicked right into police mode.

"Scarlet? What are you reading?" he said, and he took the paper out of my hand.

I, still dumbfounded, watched his eyes move over the words. I saw his jaw lock and his face turn red. He said, "NO," marched me to the principal's office, and, if I remember correctly, slammed the note down on the secretary's desk.

"I. NEED. TO. SEE. MR. GOMEZ. RIGHT. NOW."

I was still in a bit of a fog, trying not to think about the grotesque things the note said. Things I'd heard about in health class, but twisted and humiliating. I tried not to think about the part where the author of the note said he was going to hurt me.

The principal sat me down and asked me a million questions. He asked if I thought the sweet boy whose name was at the bottom of the letter had written it.

"I can't imagine he would ever do that . . ."

After more questions, I remembered the jokey guy in science class who teased me about the shy boy liking me. When the principal noticed I had a light bulb moment, he asked for a name, and I said the name out loud.

Then, I got ushered out. I heard about what happened next through the grapevine. Apparently, the guy whose name I said got called into the office, and he said, "We didn't mean anything by it. It was a joke."

And the principal said, "Who is 'we'?"

And then, the popular, beloved football player who'd actually written the note so I wouldn't recognize the jokey guy's handwriting, got called in.

And then they both got kicked out of school. Expelled. Done. Gone forever.

They had made terrible threats, but everyone blamed me.

I tried to tell people what happened. I explained I had nothing against those guys. I begged people to believe I wasn't the type who made No Talk Lunch lists anymore. I tried to convince my classmates that I didn't mean to hurt anybody. I felt so torn. The letter was not okay. And now, as a parent, thinking of my girls getting a letter like that makes my skin crawl and makes me realize I'd probably be chanting "EXPEL, EXPEL, EXPEL" into a megaphone if it was my kid.

But back then, while I was forced to sit alone in the school cafeteria, just me and my lunch-tray pizza, all I could think was *Everybody hates me. Everybody blames me. Am I who they think I am? Am I worthy of hate? Am I really the worst?*

Hear me: No one is allowed to threaten you. No one is allowed to make inappropriate comments about your body, either joking or otherwise. I knew that in that moment, and I was NOT in the wrong. But I had been many times before. I'd made lists and made waves and made judgments. And when my little world turned on me, I allowed public opinion of me to define me.

They said, "You're the worst!"

And in the quiet moments, I said, "God, I think they're right."

As a kid in a Christian school, I thought self-loathing was synonymous with humility; but self-hate is never humility. Self-hate, self-doubt, is just another form of pride. It's another form of self-obsession that leads you away from what is real and good.

Echoing a concept from C. S. Lewis, Rick Warren once said, "Humility is not thinking less of yourself; it is thinking of yourself less."[1]

Good, Good Fathers

I'm actually with my in-laws in South Carolina as I write right now, and I was telling my father-in-law about this chapter, forgetting that he wound up taking over as headmaster of the school the year after the locker note incident (yes, I married my principal's son. I didn't know he had a son at the time, but now we're married).

As I told my father-in-law what I was writing about, I remembered that every year, one of those two letter writers (I'm not sure which one) applied to return to the school. Mr. Hiltibidal (my now father-in-law) would call my dad and say, "Mr. Wessel, So-and-So's parents are requesting for their son to return to school this year."

My SWAT dad would say, "Absolutely not."

My headmaster future father-in-law would say, "Got it."

I was so wrapped up in what my peers thought of me back then that I didn't even appreciate what a gift it was to have a dad and a future dad who were looking out for me like that.

Had I been more focused on the fathers who were looking out for me and their opinions, I could have rested in that. But I was looking to the opinions of the wrong people. People who didn't completely know me and who weren't consistently "for" me.

But we all have an even better Father looking out for us. He is a Perfect Dad. He knows us fully and is more for us than our heads can understand.

Had I been focused on the opinion of my heavenly Father, I wouldn't have cried myself to sleep every night. Sure, I'd still feel sadness over the situation, but there's a peace that comes when you rest in your truest identity—the protected and loved child of a good, good Father. There's a calm, even in loneliness or conflict, when you can look beyond the lunchroom to a God who is rich in mercy because of the great love He has for us (Ephesians 2:4).

Maybe those guys spent every new school year being freshly angry with me or my dad. Maybe they felt sorry for what happened. Maybe they never thought about it again. I really don't know how that one choice they made affected them.

But what I do know is that perfect Father who I could have rested in back then loves those guys the same way He loves me. He wants to fill them with joy the way He wants to fill me with joy.

First Peter 3:18 says, "For Christ also suffered for sins once for all, the righteous for the unrighteous, that he might bring you to God. He was put to death in the flesh but made alive by the Spirit."

See, although you might classify me as the "victim" in this story, I'm certainly not "the righteous." I'm a tattle-tale. A judger. A lonely lunch eater. I'm no better than anyone I have ever hurt or anyone who has ever hurt me.

There is only One who is righteous.

All the rest of us are in the other category. Unrighteous. Me and my SWAT dad and my head-master father-in-law and those two high school boys and you and every-one you've ever met. Desperate, wicked sinners. All of us.

I'm no better than anyone I have ever hurt or anyone who has ever hurt me.

That's the thing about the gospel. Ever since Jesus ascended into heaven, people have been trying to make sense of Him through religion. But the gospel—the mes-sage that Christianity and, really, the whole world com-pletely revolves around—is different from what you see in other religions. Religion breaks the world down into two categories—good people and bad people. But if you've learned nothing else from this story, understand that those categories don't work.

To my dad, I was the good guy, and the boys who wrote that note were the bad guys. To my class, I was the bad guy, and they were the good guys. At No Talk Lunch, I thought Mario was the bad guy, and Mario thought I was the bad guy.

The gospel shows us that the real categories aren't "good people" and "bad people" after all.

My pastor, Josh Howerton, explains it this way: "Religion divides the world into good guys and bad guys. The gospel divides the world into bad guys and Jesus." Then the gospel tells us that the Good Guy died so all the bad guys could be safe.

Redefining Who You Were

So, who were you back in elementary school? Who were you last year? Were you the tattletale? The goody two-shoes like I was? Or were you more like Kristina with a *K*? And who were you three years ago? Last year?

Let me put this another way. Have you ever done something you regret? Have you ever said or done something that hurt someone? Have you ever looked back on your behavior and wished you could have done it a different way? Of course you have. We've all done dumb things. We've all been through painful things. We've all made big mistakes or been misunderstood. We all have memories that hurt our hearts and play like little movies of shame in our minds sometimes.

The lie that is so easy to believe, no matter how old you are but especially when you're young, is that you are worse than everyone around you. Watching the embarrassing memories in your mind can make you feel you are unworthy of love, of forgiveness, of good news.

But no matter what you remember about yourself and your past, and no matter how small or sad or scared you make yourself feel, if you remember the Good Father and the One Righteous, you can immediately cover over the old memories with the good news. The news that you are not who you were. In Jesus, your old is new. Your sadness is joy. Your weirdness is glory. Your loneliness is love. Because of Jesus, your past mistakes don't define you—whether you are fourteen or twenty-four or even ninety-four.

The lie that is so easy to believe, no matter how old you are but especially when you're young, is that you are worse than everyone around you.

Whether you wrote a scary locker note or a lunchtime tattle list, you are not who you were. You are not the bad things you've done.

If you have a relationship with God through Jesus, your mistakes, your reputation, even your own actions don't get to decide who you are. *Jesus does.* Jesus has.

So, Who Are You?

"But you are a chosen people, a royal priesthood, a holy nation, God's special possession, that you may declare the praises of him who called you out of darkness into his wonderful light" (1 Peter 2:9 NIV).

Jesus has decided who you are. It is set. He says, through His death, you are chosen. Royal. Holy. God's.

Isn't that wild? When you become a follower of Christ, you are not your past—you are a princess. And in case you cringe at that word, let me tell you, I'm not really the "princessy" type either.

But don't think Cinderella bedsheets and Elsa lunch boxes. Think Meghan Markle, okay? Think about a real person with real problems who suddenly becomes a real princess.

The royal thing in this verse is not just a fairy-tale pipe dream you have to abandon when you switch from Snow White sneakers to black Vans. It's your truest identity now.

I mean, just think about feeling like you couldn't be any more beautiful, any more loved, any more satisfied than you are. That's the real appeal of the whole princess thing, you know? We see the end of the stories with the perfectly smiling faces and the happiest ever afters and the news that the girl who was trapped in the tower will have glorious comfort forevermore. And we want that. It's not really about the slippers or the crowns or even the prince. We're not asking, "How does she dance so well?" We are asking, "Does she really get to be happy and safe forever?"

Jesus says to you, "Yes. You are royal. You are Mine. You will get the feeling you've been fighting for all your life."

Walking with Jesus

When I was younger, "walking with Jesus" was such an abstract idea to me. What's so great about walking?

And where are we going? Selfishly, I just wanted to know how, specifically, I could walk straight toward the things I thought I wanted, that I thought Jesus might be able to help me with. To get there, I gathered that reading my Bible was important. Praying was a thing. Doing good things was another thing (but don't take credit for them; I knew that too). But I didn't realize how simple it was to walk with Jesus and how very not about me it was.

I accepted God's grace for my ticket to heaven, but it took years for me to embrace it in the everyday. It took years for me to feel free, because I didn't know how. It took years before I got past my lunch-list shame and my school-shunning sadness.

Simply put, the Bible says that what we need to do to flee the hurt we hate and find the hope we want is love Jesus in place of loving ourselves. Or love Jesus in place of loathing ourselves.

Either way, the Bible says the main command is to love God with all your heart, soul, and mind (Matthew 22:36–37). But that can feel like an impossible thing to accomplish sometimes, right? I've asked myself, *Do I love God enough? Do I have enough heart in there? Is my soul-to-mind balance off? Am I loving Jesus the right way?*

Years later, I learned that it isn't about what I do but about embracing and believing what Jesus has already done. That's where the rest is, and that is where the love comes from. With all my heart, soul, and mind, I look at Jesus, who, in all His perfection and power, looked at me with all love as He died in my place in a real way on a real cross.

Jesus loves the Father fully and completely. And He loved you all the way to the cross and out of the grave.

Years later, I learned that it isn't about what I do but about embracing and believing what Jesus has already done.

Who are you, really, and how can you know you're doing this thing right? Look at Jesus. Talk to Him. Be diligent to read His Word. In the pages of that book, you will find who you are. You will learn who He is. You will discover that through the power of the Holy Spirit, you are capable of loving your enemies and doing good to those who hate you (Luke 6:27), even if the people who don't like you are your entire class at school.

"Love the Lord your God" doesn't feel as much like an action when you see how much He loves you (Matthew 22:37). It is a response. He loves you despite every sin you've committed, be it on a list or in a locker note. You love Him, then, because how could you not?

No matter who likes you or doesn't today, know that your Father in heaven adores you, always. And His love for you isn't based on anything you've done or even are currently doing. He just loves you. You are a princess. Even if you are a princess while eating your pizza alone.

Chapter 6

LAUGHING AT A FAKE FUNERAL

My senior year in high school, I was cast in a school play as the brokenhearted mother of a young girl who died.

It wasn't just some script our drama teacher ordered from Amazon, either. He had written it himself. It was a deeply personal story based on a student he had taught who actually did die in tragic circumstances while she was in high school.

I was supposed to be her mother. I was to perform as a grieving mom who had a difficult marriage and an ongoing battle with addiction.

In hindsight, it may have been the worst casting in the history of theater. By the time I was a senior, I felt less self-conscious and nervous and lived life bubblier and goofier. My life's work was finding the most interesting way to fix my hair and sticking backflips on the cheerleading team. Oh, and I wasn't a good actor.

This play was definitely no *High School Musical*. It was a serious, real-life drama. Even letting a smirk slip would have been highly inappropriate, not just because of the subject matter but because the subject matter was based on a true story that had so deeply affected my drama teacher that he'd written a play about it in the girl's memory.

And here's the thing: I totally respected my drama teacher, and I love the way he was choosing to honor his student's memory.

But as we all know, when you get the giggles during an inappropriate moment, there's not much that can be done about it. And my giggles came in front of a live audience as I was playing a broken addict mother of a gone-too-soon teen. And they came suddenly and with great volume.

Until that point, the play was going well. My fellow actors and I remembered our lines. The girl who played my daughter kept it together during the death scene, and we made it to the intermission. Then we changed into our black funeral outfits, a stagehand brought a real coffin onto the stage, and Juli (using her real name here because, dude, what a champion) climbed in and pretended to be a dead person.

The lights came back up, and I stood in front of my fake daughter being fake dead in a real casket, and all was going well. I didn't even need to remember any lines for this scene. All I needed to do was stand onstage and not laugh.

I had one job.

My on-again, off-again high school boyfriend was playing the pastor giving the eulogy, and another guy who was playing a fake grieving relative was standing near him. I looked at the fake relative, standing up straight in his fake funeral garb, and my eyes widened as he obviously had an itch in a zone for which standard itch protocol would recommend closed-door (not center-stage) care. Of course, he was not behind a closed door. He was correcting his problem right in front of me. And the audience.

The lights came back up, and I stood in front of my fake daughter being fake dead in a real casket, and all was going well.

I felt it bubbling up—the laughter. I knew I couldn't laugh. I absolutely couldn't. *THIS IS A FUNERAL, SCARLET.* But he kept scratching. And after a few seconds of valiantly holding it in, I unleashed laughter all over my fake daughter's fake funeral.

I look back on that moment and, I mean, I still think it's a hilarious and impossible situation. I really don't know what I could have done differently. I didn't mean to laugh. I didn't want to laugh. But I did. At the wrong thing. At the wrong time.

When People Are Punch Lines

I grew up on the set of *Saturday Night Live*. My mom was hired as a cast member when I was only six months old. It was unusual, crazy, unique. But I was the last to know that. When you're a little kid, you don't know what's unusual or crazy. All you know is your life. Whatever your life is, that's what feels normal to you. So, I grew up around the world's funniest actors. I grew up in greenrooms, riffling through gift baskets backstage at comedy clubs. In fact, on New Year's Day 2000, I was fourteen, on a stage with my mom and three former *SNL* cast members singing "Auld Lang Syne." Weird. But again, it didn't feel weird. It's only weird as I look back on it now, as an adult with a normal, non-Hollywood type of life.

So, *SNL* was my norm, and the very core of *SNL* is comedy and, really, poking fun at current events and the people who are involved in them.

We all know what it feels like to be part of a joke. It's kind of amazing, actually. In high school, I remember saying, "I love being made fun of." But what I actually meant was that I loved being part of a joke. Being part of a joke is great. You're laughing, I'm laughing, we're all laughing. Oh, the joke is at my expense? Sure! Why not! We're all having fun here. The best is when I *start* the joke about my own self. No one can hurt me that way. But what happens when it crosses a line? What happens when we go from being on the inside of the joke to being on the outside of it? What happens when everyone's laughing at us, but it's not fun; it hurts? Then it's a whole different thing. Being an outsider or, more bluntly, the butt of a joke isn't just unfortunate. It can be legitimately traumatic.

I remember being made fun of in the meaner, crueler ways. I can remember those moments in vivid detail because it was so damaging. I'm sure you can too.

It's kind of a difficult thing to try and explain.

My oldest daughter, Ever, has spent the past few years trying to figure out what sarcasm is. I tried to explain it by telling her that it's when someone says something untrue or something that they don't really mean, but they say it with a certain tone or in a certain way that conveys that it's a joke without saying, "Just kidding."

She asked me how to tell, what the tone sounded like, and I wasn't really sure what to tell her. It's hard to explain because deciphering social subtleties requires prior experience with different people and communication styles, and it requires general understanding of the world and what's true, and you're just not born knowing very much. So, you accumulate all these clues over time. We have to learn how to be made fun of.

You might notice that when people talk about this or that certain thing, and they do it in a certain tone of voice, everyone laughs. You put together that one type of thought, followed by this other type of thought, and it's funny to most people. Eventually you figure out that all that laughing can be used to hurt people.

Now, I come from a very laughter-heavy family. Growing up, the whole room would shake with laughter as we did impressions of each other. We'd invent caricatures of each other. And it was fun and fine because we were all in on it, and we didn't joke around about things that would be hurtful to anyone involved. But we have all seen that kind of humor. I'm talking about the kind of laughing and joking that cuts someone down. The kind of joking that puts a spotlight on a serious struggle or something someone is ashamed of.

When I Was the Bad Guy

Jon was on the outskirts of my friend group. He sat at our lunch table, and we talked in the hallway, but kids made fun of him. I really can't exactly put my finger on why, even thinking about it today. He had a sweet, childlike quality. He was happy looking. He didn't have that cool "I don't care about school" attitude, so that might have been what it was.

I've forgotten the exact words that were exchanged, but I'll bet he hasn't. What I'll never forget is standing outside of homeroom, close enough to the cooler kids to hear them make fun of Jon. But instead of defending him or even walking away, I turned around, faced the kids who were laughing, and joined in. I didn't notice that Jon had just walked up behind me. I was using the knowledge we all acquire about saying funny things to say hurtful things about someone who was suddenly right next to me.

There are really only a handful of times my heart has sunk like that. My stomach twisted. The look on his face.

The pain I'd caused him by the words that fell out of my mouth. It all happened too fast. I hadn't woken up that day planning on saying things that might scar one of my own friends forever. But it happened.

And there was nothing I could say to fix or undo it. Even the funniest words can't be unsaid. And the most painful words can't be wiped away.

But instead of defending him or even walking away, I turned around, faced the kids who were laughing, and joined in. I didn't notice that Jon had just walked up behind me.

I still remember his name, and he probably still remembers what I said. Not because I was someone super special in his life, but because when someone uses their words to tear you down, it sticks with you.

Being on the Other Side

The reason I'm certain that the words I've used to hurt people have the power to stick is because of the impact other people's words have had on me.

When I battled eating disorders in my late teens and early twenties, I wasn't purposely and directly thinking of the boy who saw me walk into the hallway after a summer vacation. But he said, "DANG, Scarlet. You got FAT!" and I always remembered that.

I wasn't actively reciting and reflecting on another guy's face of disgust when he saw me walk into English class in my cheerleading uniform and said, "Why are your legs so big? You have old-woman legs." But I remember.

When I was stuck in sin, a slave to my diet and dysfunction, I can absolutely trace back the insecurity that led me to the choices that enslaved me. I can trace them back to high school. Those comments about my weight, or my legs, or my Gonzo nose.

Words hurt. They've hurt me. And although I wish it weren't true, I've used them to hurt others. But in the war of words, other people are not our only enemy.

We have a deeper, truer enemy who wants to ruin us and keep us from the joy Jesus wants us to know. Satan wants us to believe that the words that have been used to injure us and the words we've used to injure others are the building blocks that shape who we are today.

Satan loves to confuse. He loves to speak lies. He's famous for twisting words. He did it when he was tempting Jesus. Remember?

> Then Jesus was led up by the Spirit into the wilderness to be tempted by the devil. After he had fasted forty days and forty nights, he was hungry. Then the tempter approached him and said, "If you are the Son of God, tell these stones to become bread."

He answered, "It is written: Man must not live on bread alone but on every word that comes from the mouth of God."

Then the devil took him to the holy city, had him stand on the pinnacle of the temple, and said to him, "If you are the Son of God, throw yourself down. For it is written:

> He will give his angels orders concerning you,
> and they will support you with their hands
> so that you will not strike
> your foot against a stone."

Jesus told him, "It is also written: Do not test the Lord your God." (Matthew 4:1–7)

Did you see that? Satan was quoting God's Word (Psalm 91:11–12) but twisting it and trying to use it to get God Himself to sin.

I mean, think back to the garden of Eden! Satan's first sentence to Eve is a direct quote from God but used in a way to attack her heart:

> He said to the woman, "Did God really say, 'You can't eat from any tree in the garden'?" (Genesis 3:1)

That's what Satan does. He twists Scripture. He takes words that are true and tries to make us believe lies. And he uses words that are lies and tries to make us believe they are true. He wants to ruin the words we need. He wants to deliver the words we don't need. He wants to bring back the hurtful words we've heard. And he wants to fixate on the hurtful words we've said.

For years, I would walk in fear and the shame of eternal condemnation. I never felt I was a good enough Christian because I knew the words I'd said. I knew the things I'd done. Even before I had such a long list of past failures, even as a child, I read the words of God and assumed they were telling me what Satan wanted me to believe—that I was cursed and would never be good enough, no matter how hard I tried.

The thing is, Satan is half-right. What has been said and done to you and what you've said and done and laughed at and stayed silent about *does* disqualify you from being good enough. Your words, his words, their words do prove you aren't enough. We can't stand under the weight of our own accusations (much less Satan's) before a holy God. But Satan has a habit of leaving out the hope . . . *Jesus saves.*

Aren't those the two best words in the world? Those two words qualify us. They make us enough. Those two words make the holy God our adopted Dad, who loves to say things to us like, "It is finished" (John 19:30), and "I have loved you with an everlasting love" (Jeremiah 31:3), and "Look, I am making everything new" (Revelation 21:5).

Who We Are

I hope that you feel some relief. I hope that you can discount lies from the enemy because you know the truth—that though we are accused and worthy of being punished, Jesus has rescued us from our sin and promised us joy.

But words still hurt. We still have to live here in the not-yet-all-the-way-new world, feeling the effects of sin on our lives.

There's an old saying that "time heals all wounds." But that's not true. I know that from experience, and I know it from looking at the experiences of people I love. Sure, things might get easier with time. But those wounds I accumulated in seventh, eighth, twelfth grade lingered in ways that manifested themselves differently as I got older. Those are still battles I have to fight.

I can chuckle about the time a friend in the locker room after PE told me I had a great personality but that my looks would never be enough to get a guy to like me. Even now, in my thirties, I sometimes find myself dressing up for an event just so other girls will think I'm pretty enough. Do you know what I mean? Like, if I know a certain woman who is really put together is going to be at something, I want to make sure I dress and look a way that she will notice. I am not even kidding you right now. Twenty years later, I don't want to be the ugly girl in the locker room. It feels ridiculous even typing that out. But words do affect us.

And the devil wants those damaging words to sink in and brand themselves into our brains and souls forever, completely defining who we believe ourselves to be right now and for the rest of our days.

But we are not defined by those words.

We are defined by *the* Word.

> In the beginning was the Word, and the Word was with God, and the Word was God. He was with God in the beginning. All things were created through him, and apart from him not one thing was created that has been created. . . . The Word became flesh and dwelt among us. We observed his glory, the glory as the one and only Son from the Father, full of grace and truth. (John 1:1–3, 14)

Who is the Word? The Word is Jesus. The Word is God Himself, the Maker of everything. And is He full of criticisms and sarcastic comments and mean jokes for us? No. What does verse 14 say that He is full of? Grace and truth.

The God who made you, the One the Bible calls "the Word," has a word for you. He has words of grace and words of truth.

But we are not defined by those words. We are defined by the Word.

His truth tells you that you need Him. It tells you that you can't be enough on your own. His grace says that you are not unlovable. You are not undesirable. You are fearfully and wonderfully made

(Psalm 139:14 NIV). We have a "we could never fix it" need, but a "the King of the world made me His daughter" answer for the need.

That is status. We have serious status. Not the kind that lasts as long as our hair looks good and our friends look cool.

Your current status is actually your eternal status if you remember the words of God about you, spoken by the Word, who created all things. Those are the words that shape and lead us. The words of guys and girls who have hurt you are not the words that matter and not the words that should be echoing in your head.

Do you know which words you need to meditate on? Not Abby's when she told you, "That sweater looks way to small to fit *you*."

No.

Meditate on the Word of God, and watch it redefine who you believe you are. Watch it change you.

That's not me talking. That's the Word Himself.

> This book of instruction must not depart from your mouth; you are to meditate on it day and night. (Joshua 1:8)

> I remember the days of old; I meditate on all you have done; I reflect on the work of your hands. (Psalm 143:5)

> How happy is the one who does not walk in the advice of the wicked or stand in the pathway with sinners or sit in the company

of mockers! Instead, his delight is in the
LORD's instruction, and he meditates on it
day and night. (Psalm 1:1–2)

Happy! You can be happy when you delight in the
words of God, rather than taking advice from the wicked
or hanging out in the company of those who use their
words to mock others.

You are a child of God. You are who He says you are.
Read, every day, about who He says you are.

So, Laughing = Bad . . . Bible Reading = Good?

Laughing is not bad. It is amazing. You'll find laughing
all over the Bible.

Psalm 126:2 says, "Our mouths were filled with laughter then, and our tongues with shouts of joy. Then they
said among the nations, 'The LORD has done great things
for them.'"

Laughter is one of the ways the world will recognize our
faith! As you learn to walk with Jesus, you'll notice the Holy
Spirit having greater power than even your own feelings.

Proverbs 15:13 says, "A joyful heart makes a face
cheerful."

We laugh because we have joy.

And sometimes we laugh because someone has the
wrong itch at the wrong time. But mostly, we laugh because
we have joy.

Chapter 7

HOPING IN HAIR-RAKING HEADBANDS

Nobody should have a mom who's a professional hairstylist when she's a teenager. It's just not fair to the rest of us. But it's a big world. So inevitably, it happens. How do I know? Because I knew that girl. I knew her, and I knew her hair. And I didn't just go to some huge school where the girl with the live-in hairstylist mom—the one who birthed her and made her hair magazine-ready every morning—only passed by you every few months.

No. My situation was different.

The person I'm here to talk about is Kate. She was *the* cool girl. No question. Her mom had disrupted the balance of the universe. Her everyday hair was just ridiculous. My hair has never in my life looked as good as the way her hair looked after PE. Not even on my wedding day. Actually, *especially* on my wedding day. I asked for loose curls, and they gave me a fifties-style bouffant underneath dozens of thick layers of hairspray. It's fine (*whyyyy?*).

So, Kate didn't just have Oscars, red-carpet-level hair. She also looked exactly like a Barbie in that weird, are-you-really-a-human way. In my memory, she was petite and blonde and perfectly Barbie shaped. Just to see if my memory serves me right, I looked her up on Facebook the other day, and at thirty-two years old, she still looks like she just walked off the page of a magazine. Anyway, whatever. Unfair advantage, but I'm so over it that I've only thought about her hair ten or twelve times this week.

My hair has never in my life looked as good as the way her hair looked after PE. Not even on my wedding day. Actually, especially on my wedding day.

She was nice enough to the people in my group, the normal-looking people group. But the problem was that all the boys liked her, and she occasionally pointed out how blue her eyes were and how blonde she was and how she still shopped in the kid section at Target because she was petite. But, I mean, if I shopped in the kid section at Target, I totally would have told you already.

Now that I'm older, looking back, I see *she* wasn't the problem. She was just the thing I assumed was the obstacle to my happiness. She got all the boys and had all the hair and the tiny, doll-sized clothes. I assumed that if she, say, got transferred to another school or had a regrettable misunderstanding with a curling iron, all the positive attention and requests to "go out" (this is what we called dating back before any of us had cars we could use to "go out" in) would naturally shift and land on, say, I don't know, ME? Maybe?

I knew I didn't look like Kate, but I was getting pretty good at drawing a light turquoise eyeliner streak across my upper and lower lids.

What I learned back then, other than how to write a persuasive paper, is that some people are told they are pretty, while others, like me, are told that they (reviewing my attributes, which we discussed in length in chapter 4) look like a boy, look weird, have old-lady legs, and/or bear a striking resemblance to Gonzo from *Muppet Babies*.

Maybe you're laughing right now at my expense. I hope so. Then there would be some silver lining to it all. Or maybe you're shaking your head and saying, "YES! I, too, look like a Muppet baby!"

Or maybe, you are THE KATE of your school. Maybe your mom is a professional hairstylist, and you are on fire.

If you're The Kate, you've probably already figured out that being The Kate is not all it's cracked up to be.

See, while I began my adolescence as a full Muppet, I eventually gained some popularity

I knew I didn't look like Kate, but I was getting pretty good at drawing a light turquoise eyeliner streak across my upper and lower lids.

and boyfriends and "status" in my upperclassman years. I guess I grew into my Gonzo nose a tiny bit, made the right friends, and figured out a way into the good circles by way of people pleasing. But it didn't take long for me to realize that "arriving" wasn't what I thought it was.

What set me up for semi-popularity was basically that a guy from the cool group had a crush on me. Once he liked me, the people in my class immediately looked at me as a new person, and soon I was at all the parties and in on all the jokes. New opportunities. Same Adam's apple.

In a way, everything changed. But in another way, nothing did.

By the age of fifteen, I realized that even when I made the cheerleading team and got the boyfriend and was crowned homecoming princess, it didn't fix the problem I had inside.

At any given moment, I was either believing I was the Muppet that didn't get cast in the movie, or realizing that looking less weird and being semipopular just weren't *enough*.

Even though the linebacker I liked asked me to his prom, why didn't he want me to be his girlfriend?

Even when the other guy I really, really liked asked me to be his girlfriend, why didn't he try to put his arm around me between classes that day? Would he like me more tomorrow? What did I need to do differently?

Even though I got invited to the big party, who's to say I'd get invited to the next one?

It was just never enough.

Wherever you are on the popularity spectrum, I think you get what I'm talking about. You want something, and the something you want feels just out of reach, no matter what you do. You stand on your tippy-toes and get it in your grasp and realize you were reaching for the wrong thing. So, you reach a little higher or a little farther for something else. You try for something more.

You think that if he just liked you, THEN you'd have it. Or if he was just kinder to you, then you'd have it. If you made better grades, had wavier hair, figured out what to do with that weird leg rash you get when you shave, then you could accept who you are. Then you could finally be admired and loved and safe and at peace.

But you can't. You and I and The Kate all know it.

Chasing those things will never give us those feelings.

Knock on the Right Door

Jesus said, "Ask, and it will be given to you. Seek, and you will find. Knock, and the door will be opened to you" (Luke 11:9). We, the seekers of shiny hair and great grades and cute boys, have some choices to make. Are we going to seek the approval of people we may not remember a year after we graduate? Or are we going to seek to know the heart of God? Are we going to seek the Word He has for us today, right now, in the situation we're stressed about? Or are we going to seek the answer on Instagram and find a skinnier/happier/smarter/funnier/whatever-looking girl instead?

Are you going to knock on the door of a guy or a friend group or a sports team that will give you that wave of the feeling you want for a second? Or are you going to knock on the door of heaven and ask the Keeper of the universe, who made the stars but still knows how many hairs are on your head, to hear what's on your heart and speak into it?

Are you going to ask God for things, relationships, achievements, status? You can't keep those things. None of them last, and needing them only leads to the sadness of your soul. Or are you going to pray for solid things? For the things that have the joy in them?

1. *Lord, will You please transform me into Your image with ever-increasing glory?* (see 2 Corinthians 3:18 NIV).
2. *Jesus, let what happens in my life be the same as what happens in heaven* (see Matthew 6:10).
3. *God, please be my shield and my glory and the one who lifts my head* (see Psalm 3:3).
4. *Do You have any wisdom for me, Father?* (see James 1:5).
5. *Can I have some of this unspeakable joy the Bible promises?* (see 1 Peter 1:8).

When you look at Jesus, chase Jesus, seek Jesus, rather than seeking status for yourself or friendship with The Kate or love from the boy, you see that He has everything that lasts. Everything that works. He has all of life, and life in abundance, and you have them too when He has you.

You have the full and complete approval of the only One who matters.

And that's not just something that old moms say to make people your age feel better. It's the truest truth there is. It's the answer to every longing you have now and every longing you'll chase as you get older.

I still find myself longing to be beautiful. I still want to be admired. I enjoy hearts on my Instagram posts just as much as the next girl. But all of it is vanity. It can't last, and it can't work.

All of it leaves me insatiable. I'm not pretty enough, not smart enough, not accomplished enough, not getting enough hearts.

Yeah, I saved up to get that pair of jeans I wanted. But what if I spill nail polish on them or they don't look as good as I think they look? Maybe I need something else too.

Or, *yeah, I have amazing friends who love me and celebrate the highs of life with me, and we mourn losses together and have so much fun. But what if I had a thousand more Instagram followers?*

Or, *losing ten pounds was great. I feel healthier and happier. But you know what might feel better than ten pounds? Twenty pounds.*

It's a never-ending pursuit. It's a never-satisfying sprint toward more. Or seen from another angle, it is a never-enough need to be worshiped.

We Want to Be Worshiped

I heard a sermon a few months ago from a pastor named Rob Turner. He was talking about how we all long to be worshiped, and when he started talking, I thought to myself, *Well, that sounds a little extreme.*

I mean, that is a goal for Lucifer. Maybe Hitler, and a few folks like that. We just want our jeans to fit, right? We just want to be able to laugh without feeling the need for nasal reconstructive surgery. But when you look back on your life and you look inside your desires, you see that it's true. We want worship.

When we're three years old, we're spinning in our most twirly dresses, saying, "Look at me! Aren't I beautiful?"

And then, we're fourteen, rolling up our cheerleading skirts, walking by the football practice and saying, "Look at me! Want me! Talk about me!"

Then, we're thirty, the age we always thought would mean our ambitions and our desperate longing for approval would be met, but now it feels more urgent than ever, and we're still saying, "Look at me! Hire me! Tell me I matter."

I just spent some time with some elderly folks in their eighties. Do you know what they said? That they felt like they were in the way. That they wanted to be helpful and needed, and they were sad because maybe they weren't.

It never ends!

As impossible as it sounds, we've got to stop thinking about ourselves. We've got to fight the pressure that we feel to conform to what our peers tell us we're supposed to be, and instead, we need to look to Jesus.

"Do not be conformed to this age," the Bible tells us, "but be transformed by the renewing of your mind, so that you may discern what is the good, pleasing, and perfect will of God" (Romans 12:2).

It makes sense that we want to conform. It feels good to belong. It feels good when people like you and admire you.

None of us wants to *say* that worship is what we're after, but it pretty much is. We want our friends to think we're amazing. We want teachers to think we're smart. We want our parents to be proud of us. We want guys to think we're the most beautiful thing they've ever seen. Right?

One Who Is Worthy

We were created to worship Jesus, not to be worshiped. We were made to reflect the beauty of the Creator in our kindness and selflessness—not produce a beauty that can be rubbed off with a makeup wipe.

It is only when you are functioning in your true identity, your identity as God's daughter, that you will truly feel approved. You will truly feel at peace. You will genuinely feel, yes, HAPPY and content.

God wants you to be happy. He totally said He wants you to have life and have it in abundance (John 10:10). And you don't need to fumble around doing it all wrong to enjoy freedom in your twenties or thirties or eighties! You can enjoy it right now. Today. Whether you're eating lunch alone in a bathroom stall or trying to decide which all-star football player's prom invitation you should accept (pick the funny one).

If you're an underdog, a late bloomer, a Muppet baby . . . how greatly can God use you to show the girls in your grade, the guys in your youth group, the parents and siblings in your house, that true beauty comes from the peace of knowing Jesus?

We were made to reflect the beauty of the Creator in our kindness and selflessness—not produce a beauty that can be rubbed off with a makeup wipe.

And if you're the "it" girl, can you imagine the impact you can have on your classmates and sisters in Christ if you choose to use the platform of popularity you've been given to point to your Maker—the Creator of your beauty and the only One who can take a pretty face and make her into a servant who makes others want the fruit of the Spirit: love, joy, peace, patience, kindness, goodness, faithfulness, gentleness, and self-control (see Galatians 5:22–23)?

Bad-Hair Years

I remember walking into homeroom one day feeling uncharacteristically confident. You see, I finally had the right plastic thing at the right time that everyone else had. It was a headband that kind of raked your hair back in a zig zag. It's hard to explain, but all the cool girls were wearing them and making them look amazing with their silky straight hair.

As I've told you, I wasn't quite sure what to do with the waves that came out of my head. This was before hair wands were invented. It was even before YouTube. I couldn't watch a tutorial. I just had a hairbrush and a picture of what I wanted in my mind. All I knew to do was blast my hair with a blow-dryer and run a brush through it. For some reason, that wasn't working for me, but what else could I do?

So, my mom bought me the rake-y plastic headband, and I thought that would cover the offense of my puff hair. So, I walked into homeroom thinking I might actually blend in, or better yet, earn a double take!

Something like, "Well, look who's here! Scarlet! That plastic rake headband that everyone else is wearing has transformed you into an instant goddess. Go ahead and pass out the trophies; we all WANT TO BE YOU. Would you sign my yearbook, or are you late for your modeling shoot?"

Instead, I was met by Kent. He *did* do a double take, but it wasn't the kind I'd hoped for.

"Scarlet . . . you look like your head got run over by a lawn mower."

Okay, so not the reaction I was looking for. It makes me laugh now, but in the moment, I was mortified.

I wanted so badly to be beautiful or even just invisible, but in the eyes of the people I wanted to approve of me, I was so ugly. They assumed I must have gotten into some sort of landscaping accident.

Has that ever happened to you? Have you ever tried really hard to be beautiful only to be humiliated? Maybe the people who humiliated you felt powerful and strong and protected from pain during the moment they hurt you, but those words they use to damage you are damaging them too.

And you can rest knowing that not only does the all-powerful, all-perfect, all-just God see all things and know all things, but if you seek Him, if you speak to Him and ask Him to speak to you in your prayer life and through His Word, you will also find that He talks to you so very differently.

You can see His great love for you in the recorded history of His actions, but because the Bible is a supernatural book, He uses those words to speak to you supernaturally, personally. And His words will never leave you mortified.

You can experience His love in that book in a way that trumps any kind of love any human person can give you.

Let Psalm 139 wash over your bad-hair day and your mean, homeroom rejection memory. God knows how many frizzy or silky or blonde or brown or black or red hairs are on your head. He knows how many pores are on your face. He made them all, and He thinks they are beautifully and wonderfully made.

Let 1 John 3:1 remind you that the world that doesn't understand God will not understand us. They will look at our hairstyles and judge us. They will look at our actions and reject us. But the Lord looks at our hearts and calls us His.

He loves what He sees—not because we have super-awesome hearts (Jeremiah 17:9 tells us our hearts are deceitful), but because our hearts have been made new.

And that may not seem to matter too much to you right now, when you just want your hair to look awesome. But think about how life really works. Think about how differently you might view your hair if you'd been born in a Third World country.

I guarantee you that the girl your age who doesn't have access to running water today isn't worrying about what her hair will look like for senior photos. She's scared of not having enough water to drink. She might be scared of dying. She's probably wondering about what happens after she dies.

And your life may feel like it is about makeup and boy drama, but we are all one car accident away from meeting Jesus. We aren't in control of how long we get to be here or even what our lives will be like while we are here, so why are we going to waste so much time on something as meaningless as our scalp coverings?

We aren't in control of how long we get to be here or even what our lives will be like while we are here, so why are we going to waste so much time on something as meaningless as our scalp coverings?

And thinking about death doesn't have to be a morbid thing when you're a Christian, because once you experience God, you know that Paul was right when he wrote, "To live is Christ and to die is gain" (Philippians 1:21).

Girls in Third World countries aren't the only ones who need an eternal perspective.

We can focus on and believe that what we possess as daughters of God, sisters of Christ, is the only beautiful identity that will last forever.

All other options are as inconsequential as hair-raking headbands.

The gospel makes us like Him now, makes us more like Him every day, and will make us like Him fully and forever.

The gospel makes us like Him now, makes us more like Him every day, and will make us like Him fully and forever.

Personality Quiz Junkie

I grew up during a weird time in history. I remember life before the internet ran the world and have experienced both sides. I completed research papers by combing through a school library, and then a few years later, I did another one and used this magical, glorious, impossible invention called Google.

I was a student when life went from feeling slow and hard and impossible to feeling instantaneous and easy and right at my fingertips.

Around this time, I discovered personality quizzes. I don't know how many hours I logged taking these things. And I don't want to be dishonest. I still take them.

Which Disney princess are you?

Will your crush ask you out?

What does your hair color say about the career you'll succeed in?

I still love a good personality test. My Enneagram number is a 3w4, and I'm an ENFP on the Myers-Briggs (INFP on a moody day). And my movie character identity is definitely Anne of Green Gables. Apparently, also, my mental age is either twenty-one or forty-five depending on which color palette I like that day.

What I'm getting at is there are lots of tools and ways you can learn about yourself. What do you like? Who are you like? What are your interests and tendencies? Those things are as easy to find out as a couple of clicks on a trackpad, but you can't actually learn about who you are or who you'll be anywhere other than in the pages of God's Word.

The gospel, the magnificent news that you are fully known and fully loved by the one perfect and loving God, not because of something you did but because of Someone who loves you, is what tells you who you'll be.

Do you think acting the right way and dressing the right way and writing the perfect essay for your college applications will determine your future? It might play into which college accepts you or what you major in, but even important things like education don't tell you who you'll be.

Rather than striving for the perfect outfit and the perfect grades and the perfect college, you can rest, knowing that you'll be made new (2 Corinthians 5:17). You can breathe, believing that He who has begun a good work in you will complete it (Philippians 1:6). You can rejoice, knowing that Jesus is currently sitting at the right hand of the Father (Luke 22:69) and that He is coming back someday (Revelation 1:7).

Who will you be? The girl in your class with good hair? The young woman at college with a promising career path? Maybe.

But your hair and your career aren't forever, and they aren't who you are. Your hair and your career don't have the power to make you feel okay with yourself. The only One who can do that is your Maker. The One who made that head of hair that you spend so much time on.

Headbands and hair days don't equal life. Jesus does.

"In him was life, and that life was the light of men." —John 1:4

Section 3

THE GOSPEL TELLS YOU WHO YOU'LL BE

Chapter Eight

JEWELRY SHOPPING AT PET SUPERMARKET

I went through a very bizarre fashion phase in high school. I was trying to figure out the meaning of life and, more important, exactly what my accessorizing was going to tell the world about who I was.

I'd say the rock bottom of my entire fashion-finding-myself phase was when I asked my mom to please drive me to Pet Supermarket (okay, maybe I was old enough to drive myself) and give me some money so I could stick it into the machine that engraved stainless steel dog-bone-shaped tags.

For the sake of clarity, those tags are for dogs. You know, to go on their collars

I'd say the rock bottom of my entire fashion-finding-myself phase was when I asked my mom to please drive me to Pet Supermarket.

with their names and your phone numbers in case they get lost?

My plan was to have my own name and my new, personal phone number engraved on the front of a dog-bone tag. I would then put the dog tag onto a black ribbon, which I'd tie around my neck like a choker. Or, if you will, like a dog collar.

Stay with me. I had a thought process about it, okay? Well, maybe I wouldn't call it a "process."

It's just that I was in this play over the summer. I tried out for a solo and didn't get one. I, along with the other less-than-skilled wannabe soloists, found our names in a big clump under "Chorus Line."

Of course, that meant we got to sing backup with the CD during the play and move our arms around in circles at the same time.

I knew it was a good casting decision not to give me a leading role. Because, you see, I wasn't good (remember: fake funeral laughing). I'm not a good singer, a good dancer, *or* a good actor. I knew I was unqualified.

And I knew the girl they picked was qualified. Somehow, she would just open her mouth, seemingly with as much effort as it would take to let out a yawn, and the most captivating sound would come out. Her voice was downright enchanting, and she was also super pretty and great at acting and, you know, good for her.

I wouldn't say I was jealous. She was so far beyond what I could ever hope to be on a stage that I was more just in awe of her.

I knew I couldn't be like her in the musical theater talent department, but as I watched her sing, my eyes locked on what she had around her neck.

Yes, you guessed it. A dog collar. Okay, not a collar, but a dog tag on a choker! Just what I needed.

I know it sounds so silly, but the moment I saw it hanging from her neck, I had to have one of my own. I needed to own and wear my own dog collar.

I didn't even furrow my brow. I didn't even think to myself, *Is that . . . a dog collar? Why is that human teenager wearing a dog collar?*

No. My subconscious was screaming, *SHE HAS SOMETHING YOU CAN HAVE! No, not the voice or the talent or the face or the perfect everything. You can't have that. But you can have that dog collar. Like, TODAY.*

I guess I wanted to be like her because she was so successful. So magnetic. I wanted people to think I was amazing. . . . I wanted to be magnetic. Maybe a dog collar would do it. Maybe, I'd get the dog collar, put it on, and feel magically infused with confidence and that je ne sais quoi the super-talented girl had. I mean, it couldn't hurt to try.

My dear mother indulged me. I was half-thrilled and half-paranoid that someone would come up behind me and say something like, "New puppy?" Maybe that did happen and I've shut it out of my mind. But mostly I was excited that day. It was one to be remembered for two reasons: (1) I was going to be like the girl. And (2) I was very proud that I'd just been given my OWN phone line, which meant I had a brand-new, only-for-me phone number to put on my shiny new dog tag.

Let me explain what that means. Back in the days before iPhones, there were these things called home phones, also known as "landlines." Maybe you've heard of them. Your grandma might have one, but probably she doesn't. My grandma is eighty-five, and she no longer has a home phone.

Anyway, there were house phones attached to the walls, and it was a very wonderful and independent thing to have your very own phone line. If you didn't, you shared the house phone with your family, and anyone from any room could carefully and quietly pick up from the other room and hear what you were saying. Or if you really wanted to call someone but someone else was on the phone, you just had to wait your turn.

So, having your own phone line felt monumental. I had a little black phone in my room with my own number that would go to my phone only. I could have private conversations with my friends, and whenever I wanted to.

The point is, I had my own number, and that was something I *did* have great confidence in. It made me feel cool and independent and free in all the ways you hope to feel when you're a teenager.

So, in my young mind, the dog collar would do the following: make me feel as electric and talented as the girl who got the part in the play AND let the world know that I, Scarlet Elizabeth, the girl who wore a dog collar, had her very . . . own . . . phone.

Whoa.

So, I got a dog collar. I remember the thrill of the silver, engraved dog bone dropping out of the machine.

And the wave of excitement I felt when I tied it around my neck.

My next memory was returning to school with it on and being met with only two reactions.

1. Some people ignored my life-altering dog collar.
2. Some people looked confused and said, "Why are you wearing a dog collar?"

I quit wearing it after a day.

The thing I thought would make me more confident did, but only long enough for me to walk from my car to my first class. That thrill of confidence I felt was shattered as soon as the thing making me confident was ignored and mocked.

Although I retired the dog collar pretty quickly, I know I spent *at least* the next decade reaching for comfort and security in places that were usually less odd, but just as unfulfilling.

Later, in high school, I looked to dating relationships. The accessories I reached for were whichever ones I thought would make the guy I was currently crushing on like me more.

But do you know what? Sometimes seeking God goes against seeking the "accessories" of life that I think will bring me comfort or excitement.

I'm learning, now, that following Him can and often does feel uncomfortable and look strange, just not in the dog-collar sort of way.

When Living for the Lord Looks Weird

When I was in the middle of the adoption process, one of my other kids got sick. And I had some trepidation about taking her to the pediatrician. You see, I really like it when people like me. And our pediatrician previously seemed to like me. But then I sent him Joy's medical files to ask his advice about her medical condition. This was when we were still praying over the decision to adopt her, and his evaluation over the phone made it clear he thought I was crazy. He spoke slowly and in a tone that I haven't been spoken to in since I was under the age of *adult,* as he explained that it didn't seem like a very wise decision.

Sometimes seeking God goes against seeking the "accessories" of life that I think will bring me comfort or excitement.

And, hey, I didn't blame him at all. Before I got into the adoption process, I probably would have used that same tone with myself. I would have given the same advice myself. Because financially, emotionally, and pretty much in every other way, adopting a Deaf and maybe mentally handicapped girl was way risky. And also, just a sort of bizarre life choice. Like, even *more* bizarre than wearing a dog collar. I get it.

Anyway, I sucked it up for Brooklyn's appointment, made a few jokes, and finally got the doctor in my corner, or at least, I got him to change his tone and agree to be Joy's doctor.

Following God to an unexpected and sometimes scary place changed me. While wearing a dog collar made me feel like an individual, adopting a needy stranger has become a daily reminder that I am a needy stranger. It is a constant reminder of the gospel. It's a constant *being put in my place.* With every phone call from our social worker, and through every doctor's appointment I take Joy to, in every moment I look up a sign I don't know so I can talk to my daughter, I'm reminded how little I'm in control and how real Jesus is.

Dog-collar-wearing me believed this bizarre lie that wearing a dog bone with my name and phone number on it would be a unique and fulfilling life choice. But it turned out to be *so* not those things.

> While wearing a dog collar made me feel like an individual, adopting a needy stranger has become a daily reminder that I am a needy stranger.

Fifteen years and zero dog tags later, I have never felt happier or more peaceful than I do right now, because when I press in to the heart of Christ, He replaces my desires for dog collars with desires like orphan care. He replaces my need to be seen with the knowledge that He already sees me.

And even a year and a half after bringing Joy home, the skeptics over our adoption are still easily found. I was getting my nails done yesterday and brought my girls. Joy saw the bright-red paint going on my nails and started telling the whole salon, in sign language, that Mommy was getting red nail polish on her nails, just like Joy had on her nails. The Vietnamese man painting my nails leaned forward and said, in his broken English, "If you were going to adopt . . . I just don't understand . . . why you adopt special needs . . . Why didn't you just adopt someone . . . how do you say . . . someone normal?"

Standing alone, that question could be taken as super offensive (especially when Joy is *with* me), but I wasn't offended, because I knew that the man doing my nails wasn't trying to insult me. He was genuinely trying to figure out why any sane person would welcome any sort of hardship into her life.

> But the person without the Spirit does not receive what comes from God's Spirit, because it is foolishness to him; he is not able to understand it since it is evaluated spiritually. (1 Corinthians 2:14)

Right there in the Bible. People can't always understand or make sense of a spiritual decision we made as a family because they don't have the spiritual eyes to see it. To them, it's foolishness.

To them, it's as foolish as a teenage girl wearing a dog collar. But it's not foolishness to the Lord.

Claire's

I remember many trips to the mall with my mom. We went pretty frequently because she always wanted to stop in the Things Remembered store to pick up engraved photo albums to give people as gifts. That was our go-to family gift. It was also the way she documented every second of our own family's life.

Happy 54th Birthday, Uncle Ben!

Cheerleading—May 2002

Oil Change—Spring 1999

Trip to Erie, Pennsylvania

Waiting in Line at Things Remembered Collection, Part Three

I'd squat beside the counter while she told the guy we saw all the time that she wanted the Old English font, as always. I think, actually, she switched to double line print somewhere in there. These were details that pained me. These were things I didn't want to think about or know about. I didn't want to be in there, staring at graduation mirror boxes and bar mitzvah canteens. I just wanted to be at Claire's. I could endure pretty much any horrible errand if I knew it would result in a five-minute stroll through Claire's.

Man, did I love Claire's. Where else could you find rainbow plastic ice cream cone necklaces? Or faux zebra fur scrunchies? Or soccer-ball–shaped change purses? Or key chain frogs with eyes that bugged out when you squeezed them? Or secret diaries with unicorn keys? From the mall store flowing with milk and honey, that's where. CLAIRE'S.

Anyway, I loved this place for years and years. I could walk in one person, and walk out with something new that would make me feel like someone I'd seen who had something I wanted. Claire's made me feel as brand-new as the bracelet that looked like it was made with nothing but hot glue for only $12.99 plus tax!

I loved Claire's well into my twenties. But now, though I wear a few Claire's-esque things every once in a while, I prefer traditional jewelry more than the glittery, plasticky, trendy things Claire's has to offer.

And, listen: I don't have very much jewelry, at all. I had a diamond engagement ring from my husband, but the diamond fell out last Thanksgiving, so now I just have a band.

When You Lose Your Diamond

It's funny. You'd think it would feel more shattering. Losing something so valuable. So sentimental. But it wasn't. Don't get me wrong; I wasn't happy about it. But after a miniature wave of loss, I was seriously *over it.* Why? Why was losing such a big thing such a small deal to me?

Because, I know that my marriage doesn't have anything to do with a shiny bauble.

See, my relationship with Brandon warrants a symbol more valuable than anything you can pick up at the Claire's in the mall, next to Things Remembered. My marriage is more precious than what they sell at the Kay Jewelers a few storefronts down from the Claire's. Marriage deserves the rarest and most beautiful stone because the love of marriage is just about the rarest and most beautiful thing! The marriage relationship is such a uniquely special picture of our relationship with Jesus.

Now, don't skim over this next part because I used the word "marriage" a lot. You might feel like marriage is a million miles away, or maybe you're not interested in getting married at all. But I think it's important to think of our crushes and dating relationships through the lens of Scripture and the way God designed male and female romantic relationships. Because if you're not looking at it through that lens now, you will devalue what's valuable and esteem what's unimportant. You'll take the fake zebra fur over the diamond.

The Bible calls the church (that's us, believers) the "bride of Christ."

When Paul was writing to husbands and wives in Ephesians, he charged husbands to love their wives as Christ loves the church "and gave himself for her" (5:25).

Jonathan C. Edwards, in his article titled "Your Marriage Is Not About You," wrote, "We've subtly come to believe that marriage is more about self-gratification and less about self-sacrifice. The apostle Paul paints a different picture of marriage in his letter to the Ephesians. Paul explains that instead of a selfish union, marriage at its core is designed to be a *selfless* union (Ephesians 5:22–27). Death to self, not personal gratification, is the center of marriage's gravitational pull."[2]

Maybe you're dating to have fun. Maybe dating is a romantic experience you're only beginning to daydream about. Or maybe you've been dating the same guy for a long time. Maybe you're talking about marriage. I was that girl, actually.

I wanted to marry my high school sweetheart so bad. I talked about it. With him. With my family. With my friends. *Oh, my poor friends.* Anyone who'd listen.

I thought love was about finding someone to love *me,* keep *me* safe, make *me* happy. I mean, dying to self didn't sound very romantic. But through years of heartache of seeking love to fill myself, I found that what I thought would work, what I thought would heal my heart, what I thought would fix me, wouldn't. It couldn't.

I heard sermons in church and got dating advice from godly people about my problem. And I'm sure they pointed me to Christ, but at the time, Christ didn't make sense to me. It was just a word that represented a person that I knew "good girls" believed in. And that's what I wanted to be. A good girl who was loved. But I kept looking for boys to love me and fill up the emptiness in my heart.

I heard glowy, happy people talking about their relationships with Jesus, and I thought to myself, *But how? What does that mean? They feel like the next Moses because they said some prayers that bounced off their ceilings? At least that's how I feel when I pray. . . .*

So, I always looked elsewhere. I looked for the guy. Then, I had the guy, so I wanted a RING. And so, I got the promise ring. But it was just never enough.

My relationship with my boyfriend was an idol. It was absolutely, clearly, embarrassingly my idol. And when said boyfriend ended our relationship, that's what he said to me. He told me that we needed to break up because I'd made him more important than God.

I responded maturely and calmly and graciously. Just kidding, I scream-cried and scream-screamed and threw my promise ring at him. Yep. I did that.

He ended our relationship, which at the time, felt like the end of LIFE.

But by the time I found Brandon and got married, the Lord had already taught me that

I heard glowy, happy people talking about their relationships with Jesus, and I thought to myself, But how? What does that mean? They feel like the next Moses because they said some prayers that bounced off their ceilings? At least that's how I feel when I pray. . . .

my high school boyfriend was right and that no guy and no ring could ever fulfill me.

Twelve years into marriage, I can tell you the ring I lost and the ring I still have, they don't really do anything. There's no power in them. Here's the thing about *things*. People? Things? Stuff? You can't find contentment there.

"Don't store up for yourselves treasures on earth," Jesus warned, "where moth and rust destroy and where thieves break in and steal. But store up for yourselves treasures in heaven, where neither moth nor rust destroys, and where thieves don't break in and steal. For where your treasure is, there your heart will be also" (Matthew 6:19–21).

I'd read those verses and think they meant that so-called contentment was supposedly found in talking to the ceiling and hoping it might talk back.

But I couldn't see God. I didn't hear a voice. So, I didn't really try. I'd open my Bible and see a bunch of words that confused me. My eyes would shift to the TV screen, where I saw happy people wearing things that looked cool, and my heart said, *Do what they're doing. Buy that outfit. Pursue that guy. Get that necklace.*

Remember Jeremiah 17:9, "The heart is more deceitful than anything else"? Yep, anything that can convince you the secret to your joy can be found in Claire's can't be trusted.

More Than an Accessory

Around the time I started obsessing about accessorizing, my dad would poke fun at me about it. When we'd pass in the house, he'd mumble, "Accessories, accessories, accessories."

To a middle-aged police officer, plastic wristbands and mood rings and choker necklaces seemed really silly. But to me, they were a comfort; they were an access point to relationships.

Maybe that sounds silly to you too, but look at your life. Do you sometimes stress about what you're going to wear? To prom? To the first day of school? On your first date? Is getting your hair and your nails and your outfit just right important to you? I'm going to submit that it is, because it often feels important to me too. It did then and it still does sometimes today.

Thankfully though, it doesn't feel as important as often. And that is because Jesus is more than an accessory we add onto our lives. He is a total makeover. He doesn't try to fit inside of whatever we are becoming. He says He IS the thing we are becoming. He doesn't want to polish you up; He wants to completely remake you. But don't freak out when you think about that, because in a real, back-and-forth, transformative relationship with Jesus, we still get everything good we are looking for. We just don't get it in the way we think we might.

143

We first experience a change that is a sort of death. And that might sound like a negative, scary thing, but it is the most beautiful scary thing ever, and it is our only hope.

I love this quote I found by C. S. Lewis because it is a strong explanation of this. Lewis wrote, "Christ says, 'Give me All. I don't want so much of your time and so much of your money and so much of your work; I want you. I have not come to torment your natural self, but to kill it.'"[3]

Christianity is not putting on a Claire's bracelet; it is picking up a cross. We are not first prettied up; we are first broken down. We are not tweaked; we are crucified.

> Christianity is not putting on a Claire's bracelet; it is picking up a cross.

"I have been crucified with Christ," wrote Paul, "and I no longer live, but Christ lives in me. The life I now live in the body, I live by faith in the Son of God, who loved me and gave himself for me" (Galatians 2:20).

The key to the happiness we want is not found in being cuter than we are now. The happiness we want is found in being "crucified with Christ." That is because when we die to ourselves through Him, we find that the life we were designed for is in Him. We don't become better versions of ourselves; we become little versions of Jesus. Every day, whether we feel it or not, God is making us more and more like Him. More and more glorious like He is glorious.

See, Jesus doesn't want to ruin your life and make you miserable. He wants you to abandon your hopes and replace them with His. He hopes for you to be like Him and every day have a little more of life—and life to the fullest—that being like Him brings (John 10:10).

The gospel gives you a newness. Every day. Look: tomorrow you will be a little more like who God says you already are in Jesus. You will think a little more like He says you are in Christ. You will feel a little more like He says you do in Christ. The gospel gives you a different future. One where each day you are a little more secure, a little more at peace, a little less concerned about your jewelry or the number of banana chips you eat. The Bible says that we are being transformed into the image of God from glory to glory, a little at a time, but all the way to the end (2 Corinthians 3:18).

The gospel, then, always gives us a future identity—not just a future as a mom or as a wife or as a president of a bank or something. We have a future-future, an after-that future, in the new heaven and new earth (see Revelation 21). We have the hope of a little more joy in Jesus tomorrow. And we have the hope of everything joyous in Him forever.

See, Jesus doesn't want to ruin your life and make you miserable. He wants you to abandon your hopes and replace them with His.

Pursuing and enjoying that reality is something that requires a daily fight—a fight against pursuing uniqueness for the sake of uniqueness, or uniqueness for the sake of being exalted. But what does uniqueness matter when we are being made like God? And what exaltation can you find onstage at a school play that can compare to reigning with God forever and ever?

"This saying is trustworthy: For if we died with him, we will also live with him; if we endure, *we will also reign with him*; if we deny him, he will also deny us; if we are faithless, he remains faithful, for he cannot deny himself" (2 Timothy 2:11–13).

Hold on to your headbands, friends. We aren't just princesses; we are destined to be queens. Tell that to the mirror tomorrow.

So we don't need what we can find at Claire's or Tiffany's or Pet Supermarket. Our peace, our future, our very identities have been purchased already, by the blood of Christ. They have begun already as we become like Him. We can rest in that, knowing that we absolutely and beyond our wildest dreams have everything we need. Dog tags not included.

Chapter 9

I CHANGED MY NAME
TO SANDY

I used to get really jealous of people with nicknames. When I was in school, any girl in my class who'd shortened her name and added a *y* to the end had something I really wanted. It wasn't about the *y*, but more about the casual confidence that the *y* represented.

Hi. I'm Mandy.
Oh, hello. My name is Jenny.
Me? Oh, nice to meet you. I'm Abby.

I wanted to feel casual and confident, but Scarlet can only be shortened to "Scar," which doesn't really work. And if you add a *y* to *Scar*, it becomes "Scary," which *definitely* doesn't work.

Just to frame this correctly, I'm now going back in time, pre-boyfriend, pre-hair-that-made-sense-for-a-human, back to the version of myself that had exactly one friend.

During those earlier teen years, I was so the opposite of cool that even the teachers made fun of me.

Flashback:

The dean walks into the room to check that the girls are dressed appropriately for picture day.

"Good morning, students! I'm here to make sure everyone is dressed modestly and according to school standards since today is dress-up day. Specifically, I am going to make sure that no one's skirt is too short *[looks at my floor-length "Little House on the Prairie" gown with actual petticoat underneath]*. Oh, Scarlet, I think we're going to need to call your parents."

Other flashback:

(Me to my best [only] friend, Vicky) "Vicky—I touched Joey's hair today! We were standing in line, and he had a speck in his hair and I brushed it off!!!"

Okay, now that you have a better idea of who I was at the time this happened, let me tell you about an incident in Miss Mendez's computer class one day. I was so tired of feeling awkward and uncool. I knew if I had a catchy nickname, like the cool girls and like my friend Vicky, I'd feel the confidence I lacked and become cool, or at least more comfortable.

So, Miss Mendez paced around the computer lab and said, "Okay, class. We're going to play a new typing skills game! I'm going to guide you into the program, and we'll get started! First step—type your first name into the box on your screen that says 'name.'"

This was my moment. I knew it. This was it. This was my chance for the casual. This was the time for the confidence. Today, I was getting my *y*.

My heartbeat sped up as I stared at the keyboard and the opportunity before me.

I rested my fingers over the keys and typed, "S-a-n-d-y."

I felt a surge of electricity enter my body, like I'd gained a superpower.

SANDY.

I tried to stifle the smile that threatened to expose itself, because surely cool people with names like Sandy wouldn't smile in such situations. They would lean back and be all Sandy-ish. *Uh, of course my name is Sandy. Can't you tell? Maybe you noticed my crossbody black leather fanny pack?*

But before I even got past trying not to smile and into figuring out how I would go from having a fake name on a computer screen to making my entire class think it was completely normal to go from calling me "that weird girl with the floor-length strawberry-print gown" to "Sandy," my teacher's voice boomed (maybe in slow mo), "Let's see who's following directions."

Please walk away. Please walk away. Please walk away. She circled the room like a vulture and, as fate would have it, stopped right in front of my chair.

Please walk away. Please walk away. Please walk away.

She circled the room like a vulture and, as fate would have it, stopped right in front of my chair.

I looked through her, as to avoid eye contact.

"Scarlet! Tell me . . . what did you type in the box where it says 'name'?"

Seriously? Is God punishing me for telling on the kids in No Talk Lunch?

"Um . . . I typed . . . Sandy?"

I am so serious when I tell you that I have no idea how the story ends. All I know is that I felt like I was going to throw up and die and explode and be shot out of a cannon into outer space and then fall back down to the earth, but I wouldn't have fallen back onto a soft place. It would be like in the center of an erupting volcano. Maybe that's what actually happened and that's why I don't remember anything. Who knows?

All I know is that "Sandy" didn't stick. Thirty-two years in, and I am still full-blown Scarlet. I've lived so much life, but my name still ends in a *t*.

I don't know. What I do know is that I genuinely believed that having a catchy name would bring me some sort of happiness and some level of approval. My plan backfired, but of course, even if it had somehow worked out and I had convinced everyone I was cool and casual Sandy, whose skirts never dragged on the floor, I would have still been unsatisfied.

But I am not Sandy. I'm not even Scarlet. I am completely united with Jesus. His identity is my identity. And His name doesn't need a *y* to be beautiful.

I know from experience that viewing myself as a Christian is the only time I feel the humble confidence that brings peace.

Living in that identity is the only way I'm capable of looking at the girls with cool names and thinking, *How can I serve them?* instead of *How can I be them?*

> *Living in that identity is the only way I'm capable of looking at the girls with cool names and thinking. How can I serve them? instead of How can I be them?*

The Popularity Puzzle

When I was younger, I didn't yet have analytical skills to figure out why the popular girls were what they were, why people liked some people and made fun of others. So, I looked on the surface. I looked at their appearances. I looked at their hair and their clothes and even their names.

"Humans do not see what the LORD sees, for humans see what is visible, but the LORD sees the heart" (1 Samuel 16:7). That was so true of me back then.

I saw *y*'s at the ends of names on the papers beside me. I saw chokers and rake-style hair bands and skirts that were dangerously teetering on the borderline of the two-inches-above-the-knee dress code. I assumed that's what made the girls I did life with socially successful.

And because I did life with a bunch of humans like me who were looking at the visible, rather than the invisible, I was maybe a little bit right. Being trendy and having things that everyone on TV had might have felt like it was helping for a moment. But as any older, wiser person will tell you, the coolest kids, the trendsetters, the ones who set the tone at your school for what is cool are often the ones who have confidence. They're the ones who appear to be having fun. They're the ones who seem relaxed. They're the ones who look like they have thick skin and can shrug off a harsh comment or a detention like it's NO BIG DEAL.

So where does their confidence come from? Maybe it *does* come from some material thing they have. But you and I know (or you will know) by experience that any material thing or even any person that makes you feel secure will let you down eventually.

You can try to have their confidence. You can try to "fake it 'til you make it," as the old saying goes. Or you can buy the things they have (see dog collar, chapter 8). You can mingle with cool people or date the right guy. And you'll discover the age-old truth—that a confidence built on flimsy things is a confidence that won't hold up.

Confidence is a thing you can have. But you can keep it only if your confidence is built on something sturdy enough.

Buying a House with a Bad Foundation

I grew up in apartments, town houses, and suburbs. Country life was a foreign concept to me, but I grew up and married a man with a country side to him (even though when I met him, he played electric guitar and wore a leather choker with a guitar pick strung around it, because he is a lot like me, including our matching Adam's apples).

Anyway, we spent most of our life in apartments, but last spring we decided to move to the outskirts of town, where we could have some land and animals.

Let me just say up front, we had twenty chickens and none of them lived, and now we are farmers with no plants or animals. But that's probably a conversation for a different book.

So, when we decided to move, we zeroed in on a pretty house on a hill. It was beautiful and charming and sitting on some acres, and we fell in love with it right away. We got under contract and went into the inspection phase, only to get some bad news.

Although the house looked beautiful on the outside, there were some major problems underneath, like I'm talking some $30,000 problems underneath.

The foundation was cracked in such a way that the inspector said the kitchen could cave in at any moment.

We got out of our contract and set our sights on another house because of course we knew that even if our house looked awesome, if it wasn't built on a solid foundation, it wouldn't be a place we could live in for long. It would end up being a pile of rubble.

The house we *did* buy is old, and the inspection did show signs of a prior foundation problem, but the previous owners had it taken care of. Underneath the house I'm sitting in right now are giant metal beams. The inspector said this house was set to stand firm forever, because the foundation is built on strong things. It's secure.

Jesus talked about houses and foundations when He was here on earth too.

In His famous Sermon on the Mount, Jesus said:

> Therefore, everyone who hears these words of mine and acts on them will be like a wise man who built his house on the rock. The rain fell, the rivers rose, and the winds blew and pounded that house. Yet it didn't collapse because its foundation was on the rock. But everyone who hears these words of mine and doesn't act on them will be like a foolish man who built his house on the sand. The rain fell, the rivers rose, the winds blew and pounded that house, and it collapsed. It collapsed with a great crash. (Matthew 7:24–27)

See that? That doesn't just go for farmhouses where chickens go to die. And you know what's crazy? It doesn't just go for your moment of salvation either! When I was younger, even as a young adult, I thought that the moment

I chose to follow Jesus was the only spiritual moment that mattered and that the rest of my life needed to be a daily striving to win His favor.

But the Christian life isn't about a single moment. It's not about our own efforts. It's not about striving daily as much as it is about dying daily. The Christian life is about *resting* daily in the finished work of Jesus. It's about settling into the home He's continuing to build every day in our lives. If we trust that He, not our goodness, is the foundation and that He, not our effort, is the builder, we will be at peace, and that peace will give us the confidence we need to get through our day-to-day.

The Christian life is about resting daily in the finished work of Jesus.

Right now, your day-to-day looks a little different than mine does, but not much, really.

We all want to feel safe and loved. Jesus says we are.

Better Names

All over the Bible, you can see God renaming people. He does a work in someone's life, or He gives them a mission to pursue, and tells them they have a new name. God takes people and leads them to pursue new, kingdom-centered identities, and then He makes their new names reflect that. After you read these, I encourage you to look up the meanings of these new names. For example, in the first verse I'm about to list, the name *Abraham* means "father of many." God renamed people and would often explain the reason behind it. The name changes weren't arbitrary. They had meaning.

Here are some examples of God changing people's names:

"Your name will no longer be Abram; your name will be Abraham, for I will make you the father of many nations." (Genesis 17:5)

"God said to Abraham, 'As for your wife Sarai, do not call her Sarai, for Sarah will be her name." (Genesis 17:15)

"'Your name will no longer be Jacob,' he said. 'It will be Israel because you have struggled with God and with men and have prevailed.'" (Genesis 32:28)

We see it in the New Testament as well. Saul, murderer of Christians, became the apostle Paul, who spent the remainder of his life preaching the gospel with fearlessness and joy.

And did you know that Jesus has a new name for you? The gospel says we already have names that can offer us supernatural confidence. And I checked. The name "Sandy" is not on the list.

Jesus' names for you look more like *Forgiven, Beloved, Anointed, Approved Forever,* and—get this—*Worthy.* I mean, look at that. We all get a name that ends with a *y.*

Because of the gospel, we don't have to walk in shame or search for fake names. Jesus has already called us His own.

Even more, Revelation 2:17 tells us that we will all get new, truer names someday. Not names given to us by flawed parents, but deep names given to us by our perfect Maker. Just wow.

> "Let anyone who has ears to hear listen to what the Spirit says to the churches. To the one who conquers, I will give some of the hidden manna. I will also give him a white stone, and on the stone a new name is inscribed that no one knows except the one who receives it."

Not only do you get a new name, but it's a new, *secret* name on a white stone. I love what this says about our relationship with the Lord. Have you ever had a secret with someone? A special secret? Maybe it was an inside joke. Maybe you can say the word "pomegranate" and erupt with laughter when you're with your best friend because the two of you do so much life together and something funny happened involving a pomegranate. So now, all you have to do is mouth "pomegranate" and you know and she knows that you have a special connection.

I love that God, the Existing One who has always been and always will be, desires to have a special, personal relationship with each of us. One day He is going to give us special, secret names! One day He might walk up to you and whisper, "Pomegranate." So cool.

Practical Ways to Press In

So, what can we do to stop compulsively chasing after the names that won't fulfill us? What can we do to rest in our new, God-given, always and forever identities?

I think you and I need to do the same things. I think we need to "do life with" the Lord. Walk with Him. Talk with Him. Not just as we drift off to sleep, post-Instagram scroll. I mean we need to take our prayer lives more seriously. I think we need to communicate with Him like He's our best friend, because He really is. I think we need to make prayer pour out of us like a song that's stuck in our heads. The Bible calls this praying "without ceasing" (KJV). Or, in the CSB, it is praying "constantly."

> Rejoice always, pray constantly, give thanks
> in everything; for this is God's will for you
> in Christ Jesus. (1 Thessalonians 5:16–18)

And we need to look to our ultimate example in Jesus and pray like He did. How did He pray? Well, for one thing, He often did it alone: "Very early in the morning, while it was still dark, he got up, went out, and made his way to a deserted place; and there he was praying" (Mark 1:35).

We've talked a lot about reading God's Word, but that is of course a huge part of this. As we keep reading about who He is and who we are in light of who He is, we know the names by which we are called. We know what we are becoming.

It's like being hungry and reading the menu at Chick-fil-A. The more you think about the waffle fries, the more you want them and the more convinced you are that you're going to have them. Read about who God is making you to be, and you'll see the glory and want it more.

What else can we do? Pursue friendships with other believers who are chasing after the Lord.

> And let us watch out for one another to provoke love and good works, not neglecting to gather together, as some are in the habit of doing, but encouraging each other, and all the more as you see the day approaching. (Hebrews 10:24–25)

Friends are so important. I try to keep my friends near enough to notice when my humility starts morphing into self-sufficiency and pride, and I keep returning to the truth often because they lead me there. Usually, the way they lead me is by example. I see their lives up close, and it makes me desire to be more like the Christ I see in them.

You may be young, but you can do this, Worthy with a *y*. Where can you find people who spur you on to walk in keeping with your newest, truest names? Look at youth group. Look at church. Look at Sunday school. Look at your family. Talk to people in your school, and be bold about your desire to grow spiritually. Pray for those friends. God loves to give us good gifts when we are praying for things that draw us nearer to Him.

If you abide in me, and my words abide in
you, ask whatever you wish, and it will be
done for you. (John 15:7 ESV)

I love that verse, because despite how some people
twist it, God's not saying He's a genie in a lamp, here to
grant you three wishes. He's saying that if you abide in
Him, you will know more about the things He wants. You
will ask more for the best things, the things He wants you
to have. I dare you to ask God, in faith, for friendships that
help you grow spiritually, and see what He does. I know my
God, and I know He is not only urging you to pray that
prayer, but He will be faithful in answering it too,
unleashing His blessings on you.

> I dare you to ask God, in faith, for friendships that help you grow spiritually, and see what He does. I know my God, and I know He is not only urging you to pray that prayer, but He will be faithful in answering it too, unleashing His blessings on you.

Then, He takes all those things—your desire for Him,
your walking with Him, your talking with Him, your
reading about Him and yourself, your fighting for joy in Him
with your people—and He slowly but surely makes
you into what He has already named you. He shapes you into what

you will be forever. You will feel it. You will see it and walk more confidently than you've ever dreamed. You can push through life with the how-can-this-be hope that you have a secret name and a perfect glory coming to you on the other side of the grave. The One who conquered the grave is your Dad, and He has said it will be. He says it to you, and He says it to me.

And I hope it's okay that when I imagine Him passing me my secret white stone, the name He has chosen is "Sandy."

Chapter 10

DOING BACKFLIPS AFTER A TEN-YEAR HIATUS

A few months ago, I was at my mom's house, watching home videos from years past. We watched a few videos of my sister and me performing a show that has become infamous in our family. Yes, you guessed it—I'm talking about *The Cindy Sparkles Show*.

There's actually no way you guessed it, because *The Cindy Sparkles Show* was something we made up and performed in a two-bedroom, rented apartment for one audience member, and that audience member was my mom.

In the show, I, acting as a famous yet clearly unskilled "magician," sang a made-up, stream-of-consciousness song, complete with instrumental solos comprised of only my very own unpleasant-sounding voice. Meanwhile, my a-sister-sistant (that's a sister who is also an assistant), Aubrey, who was three years old, talked into a plastic Diet Coke bottle as a microphone. I still remember her monologue.

"Everyone loves me . . . in a special way. So, if you wanna get it, come on and DIT IT!"

Her *g*'s still sounded a little bit like *d*'s sometimes. Also, I still don't know what she meant by that. *Cindy Sparkles* is one of our core family memories because it was SO poorly executed, and my sister and I were SO oblivious to that. The combination of those two things made home movie magic.

I'm so glad it exists on video. If I were able to somehow put a streaming video player on this paper book page, I would show it to you.

LONG LIVE *CINDY SPARKLES*!

Anyway, I enjoyed performing poorly put-together magic shows in my youth, but then I got older and realized that performing things that were actually good was a way better use of my time.

GO, DADE, #1

Except for the one year I lived in California, the school I went to was in Miami-Dade County, so I have about a million cheers saved in my brain that say things about "Dade."

D-A-D-E, Dade, Dade . . .

GO, GO, G-O, OH YEAH, GO, DADE, GO!

I'll be saying those chants in a nursing home someday. (Family, if you are reading this, now is a good time to talk about my as-yet-unmade end-of-life plans.)

I remember trying out for the cheerleading team in eighth grade and realizing that on a scale of one to ten, I was the worst, most unskilled cheerleader candidate out there. The girls trying out before and after me had toe touches that made me want to cry. Masterful. Exquisite.

Their legs were perfectly straight and hyperextended past their arms when they put their arms out parallel. Mine looked like a penguin trying to fly while stretching its flippers and tiny penguin feet as far as they'd go to each side. It wasn't pretty.

But I wanted to get it. And not just get it—I wanted to be *the best* at it.

So, I did whatever any other girl who had a dream of being a champion cheerleading toe-toucher would do. I devoted every spare second of my life to getting good. I would watch TV in a full split or while doing toe touch after toe touch after toe touch after toe touch. I'm pretty sure every girl in my grade who tried out made the team that year, so I was on the team, even though I was unskilled. But I was determined to be good. I stayed after school for cheer practice, and there was a season where I'd then also stay after practice to run a mile so I could get my stamina up.

I took it seriously because the girls around me took it seriously. We had coaches who were former competitive cheerleaders who also took it seriously. So, surrounded by peers and adults who treated cheer practice like Navy boot camp, I fully surrendered to the cheer curl and White Rain hairspray and weight room and daily practice regimen.

And I went from being an unskilled wannabe cheerleader to a very skilled, very intense competition cheerleader in one year.

In my casual life (if I even had a moment that felt casual), I wore a T-shirt that said, "Cheerleading Is Life." And I meant it.

In my casual life (if I even had a moment that felt casual), I wore a T-shirt that said, "Cheerleading Is Life." And I meant it.

Looking back on those years, 98 percent of my memories involve cheerleading in some form. I was a two-time national champion cheerleader. MAN, were we proud of those championship rings. I didn't even order a senior ring. Why would I when I had one that was so much more meaningful? (I lost them immediately after graduation, so . . .)

Please enjoy this sampling of a rap my friends and I made up on the bus going home from a competition we won.

> *Hit me with a beat . . . boom-bu-dop-boom-bop-bop, boom-bu-dop-boom-bop-bop . . .*
> *Look at the ice, look at my fingas, look at the cheerleaders, look at the ring-ahs . . .*
> *boom-bu-dop . . .*

I share the world's worst rap with you because I've learned to bring my shameful things into the light in order to walk in freedom. :)

We were good at cheer things and blaringly cocky about how good we were.

We were like robots, toe-touching until our legs about popped off.

We all had our little areas of expertise. Jessi was our world-class flyer. She full-twist cradled and landed every basket toss like a machine. Ally was the dancer. No matter how perfectly the rest of us knew each motion, Ally was the center of attention as the electronic music with strategically placed "wa-bam" and "wa-pow" sound effects pumped through our little black boom box. Molly and Cat were the bases everyone wanted because they were fearless, and their muscles were made of solid rock, and they always, always made sure the flyer didn't hit the floor.

What was my job on the team, you ask? I was a tumbler.

I'd spent a few years doing gymnastics, so I was responsible to bring the flips. I was primarily focused on hitting my mark, doing my tricks well, and making the appropriate theatrical, corny faces to go with it.

I don't know if this is still a thing, but on the days practice got rained out, we would line up in front of the lockers inside and have stage face practice.

What was stage face practice? I'll tell you. Basically, we would say our cheers over and over while doing the largest, most cartoonish, most embarrassingly giant "happy" facial expressions, meant to be seen by the judges who sat light-years away from the competition stages. We looked ridiculous, yes. But we went for it.

Yes, my time and sweat and adolescent passion were razor focused on a skill set that had exactly no practical purpose once I left high school. But it taught me about hard work and it taught me about teamwork and it taught me how to use a curling iron and smile even after my face went numb.

There Actually Was an "I" on My Team

You know the saying, "There's no *I* in *TEAM*?" Well, I sure spent my years as a cheerleader like there was.

I was really bad at what we cheerleaders called "stunting"—the thing where we throw each other into the air and catch and lift. I hated it. I didn't want to get my teeth knocked out.

So, I was good at flipping by myself and bad at working with the rest of the team. In the first couple of years, my coaches would try to challenge me by having me spot the girls who flew in the air. The first time I spotted, the flyer landed on her back and sprained her elbow. The second (and last) time I was asked to spot, our star flyer landed on her coccyx. I didn't jump backward and away, covering my face while my teammates were falling to their death, on purpose. But I did jump backward and away, covering my face while my teammates were falling to their death. It was instinctive self-preservation!

I know. I was the worst.

Back then, I loved the buzz of being on the team, but I enjoyed the most isolated role. This wasn't only a cheerleading thing for me. It was also, really until the last few years, how I functioned in relationships.

As a cheerleader, I liked wearing the team uniform, but only if I could do my own thing and not be dependent on anyone or have anyone dependent on me. In life, I always wanted to be at the party, but you could count on me having to go to the bathroom or slipping out the back door as soon as you went from small talk to deep talk.

This tendency led to me hurting a lot of people. I'd be friendly, they'd misconstrue my friendliness for genuine openness and love, and I would either fail to meet their expectations as a friend or tell them up front, "Hey . . . let's not even go where you're going, because I'm going to fail to meet your expectations as a friend."

Living this way wasn't good for them, and it wasn't good for my soul either. I thought I was okay because my life had always been very busy and full. But I wasn't growing. I wasn't allowing God to use me to do anything in anyone's life, and I wasn't letting others be used by God in my life. When I realized that fact and felt bad, I would fight the guilt by distracting myself with more busyness.

I was functioning on the team as part of it, but I wasn't actually risking my own clavicle for the safety of my friend's coccyx.

During the years I cheered, I definitely wasn't letting the gospel change me. I'd say my pattern of selfishness carried over and shaped me instead, and as a young adult, I was selfish with my time and isolated from other people.

That's such a common thing. What you do now, the patterns you're starting to form in your teen years, will shape who you become. And if you're leaning into any urges that aren't led by the Holy Spirit, you're going to find your future self struggling with problems that you can trace back to right now. You'll look back and say, "There. That's when it all started."

Being just enough part of the team of humanity, but mostly isolated, was my pattern until the last few years. I joined a small group at my church a couple of years ago, but instead of staying at arm's distance, I actually got involved in these people's lives and let them into mine, little by little. When I was afraid to do something I knew God wanted me to do, I would tell this group instead of hiding it. I would confess it instead of justifying it. I would ask them to pray.

This is what the Bible tells us to do as believers. We need to live lives of confession, live lives in community, live lives of selflessness. Check out these words of wisdom from God's Word:

> "Therefore, confess your sins to one another and pray for one another, so that you may be healed." (James 5:16)

> "The one who conceals his sins will not prosper, but whoever confesses and renounces them will find mercy." (Proverbs 28:13)

"Carry one another's burdens; in this way you will fulfill the law of Christ." (Galatians 6:2)

"If we walk in the light as he himself is in the light, we have fellowship with one another, and the blood of Jesus his Son cleanses us from all sin." (1 John 1:7)

I'd already experienced the power of confessed sin with my eating disorder ordeal in college, but I still didn't live a lifestyle of openness. I didn't enter into people's burdens, and I certainly didn't let them very far into mine.

What I found in this small group, though, was that doing the opposite thing than I'd done in cheerleading wasn't as scary as I'd thought. Instead of isolating myself to tumbling and not doing the hard work of lifting and spotting and helping, I tried to open up and get to know their lives. To my surprise, the people in my group didn't bulldoze my walls and force their way into my life. They actually didn't ask anything of me at all. They just lived like Jesus in front of me, and that changed me and compelled me to put my defensive arms down. I let them in and entered into their lives more and more because the gospel started to reshape me.

Their Christlikeness caused me to notice my own un-Christlikeness and want what they have.

"Iron sharpens iron," we read, "and one person sharpens another." (Proverbs 27:17)

Letting myself be fully on a team with a group of people—tossing and catching and praying and diving under the person who is falling and letting them catch me when I fall—has proven to be such an extreme joy.

I'm now learning that the gospel is so powerful that it can reshape a heart that's been shaped by the wrong things for years and years and years. It's just miraculous.

A Thirty-Year-Old Throwing a Tumbling Pass

Two years ago, I was at a park with my husband, Brandon, and our two daughters (Joy was still in China). He was pushing our youngest on the swing, and I'd just spontaneously dyed my hair red from a box of dye at CVS, so I was feeling extra fiery. I looked at the open field behind the swing set and smiled at Brandon. "I'm going to throw a round-off back handspring. Right there. Right now."

He scrunched up his eyebrows and questioned me, saying something like, "But you haven't done that in, like, over ten years . . . You haven't done cheerleading since I met you. Also, you haven't worked out or even stretched in a really long time."

I thought through what I'd done so many times on the hard basketball gym floor and smirked the self-assured smirk that can only be channeled by a former two-time national champion cheerleader.

"Oh. I don't need to stretch. Video me."

Out of shape and many years removed from my last decent stretch, I ran into the grass and did it. A round-off back handspring!

If you look up the video on my blog, you'll see me land it and then fall over sideways. And then Brandon started laughing. And then he apologized on the video for laughing. And then, I wore a knee brace for a month. I'm not even kidding you right now.

Is it Proverbs 16:18 that says something like, "Pride goeth before a thirty-year-old doing a back handspring, and a haughty spirit before a knee brace"?

Something like that.

After ten years of being right side up, I did a backflip and realized just how much I've changed since the last time flipping was part of my life. No longer am I the nervous show-off doing whatever it takes to keep everyone on my team at a safe distance. Now, I'm a nervous show-off who does life with people who make me want to be less like me and more like Jesus.

No longer am I the nervous show-off doing whatever it takes to keep everyone on my team at a safe distance. Now, I'm a nervous show-off who does life with people who make me want to be less like me and more like Jesus.

Who You Were, Who You Are, and Who You'll Be

What I want you to take away from this book is that no matter what you've done or where you've been, because of the cross, you can live with hope of a perfect future. And that is literal. You will be made perfect in the future. For real.

> I am sure of this, that he who started a good work in you will carry it on to completion until the day of Christ Jesus. (Philippians 1:6)

> Dear friends, we are God's children now, and what we will be has not yet been revealed. We know that when he appears, we will be like him because we will see him as he is. (1 John 3:2)

> Blessed be the God and Father of our Lord Jesus Christ. Because of his great mercy he has given us new birth into a living hope through the resurrection of Jesus Christ from the dead and into an inheritance that is imperishable, undefiled, and unfading, kept in heaven for you. (1 Peter 1:3–4)

Because Jesus is perfect and because He died in your place, the Lord sees you right now as perfect AND when you get to Him you will truly be perfect. Christ is in your place today and forever.

One day, our ever-patient, ever-present God will fix this broken world, and He will make you and me and the whole wide world perfect—without sin, without shame, without a single flaw.

> For I will create a new heaven and a new earth; the past events will not be remembered or come to mind. (Isaiah 65:17)

Oh my goodness, can you imagine? If your past events were not remembered? If they never even came into your mind? That's our future reality!

Because of Jesus, because of the good news of the gospel, who you'll be isn't something you need to stress about. You don't need to worry and waste energy trying to find the perfect boyfriend and the perfect major and the perfect first apartment. Your path will be a flawed one, but it's leading to a good place, because it's leading you closer and closer to Jesus.

You don't need to worry and waste energy trying to find the perfect boyfriend and the perfect major and the perfect first apartment. Your path will be a flawed one, but it's leading to a good place, because it's leading you closer and closer to Jesus.

Thank the Lord I am not who I was twenty years ago. I'm not even who I was one year ago.

I'm not who I will be forever, and that forever has already been secured on the cross.

Friend, there is freedom in falling short, because we have a future that won't fall short.

No matter how clear our skin is looking today, no matter who in our class or at our job or in our family likes us or doesn't, no matter how long it's been since we committed that last sin or what sin we will commit in the future, we are free. We are forgiven. We have bright, beautiful futures because of Jesus.

Jesus died to set us free from our failures—yesterday's, today's, and tomorrow's. We can rest in this and live for Him—the only way of living that will make us happy.

The me of years past no longer exists. Apparently, I can't do any flips anymore without having to go to the doctor. And listen: the you of yesterday and even the you of tomorrow won't exist anymore in the glorified kingdom God is taking us to. God isn't interested in your best flips or your straight A's or your perfect boyfriend. All He wants is your heart. All He wants is for you to let Him love you, for you to see yourself the way He sees you—completely covered by the Word of Jesus and completely loved, not because of anything you've done before or any skill you can still do, but because of what He did on a cross.

So put the makeup down, or don't, but don't let that be what your life is about. Don't call the boy, or do, but hear everything he says as a princess who will one day reign with your One True Love. Don't waste any more time rereading that Instagram message that makes you feel rejected. That's what Delete buttons are for. Jesus wants you to be full of joy—not full of regrets or full of fears.

You're not a hottie list maker; you are a beloved daughter of the only God. You are not a body you wish were different. You are hidden with Jesus, and His glory is yours. You and I are not headband wearers or test takers or back flippers with bad knees. We are "a chosen race, a royal priesthood, a holy nation, a people for his possession," so that we may proclaim the praises of the One who called us out of darkness into His marvelous light (1 Peter 2:9).

You don't need to think about your pores or boys or the time you were shunned by your friends. Instead, turn your eyes upon Jesus. Look full in His wonderful face. Then grab some waffle fries or a lunchroom pizza slice and remember what He has made true in you. You are rescued. You are wanted. You are free forever, and you are free today.

ABOUT THE AUTHOR

Scarlet Hiltibidal is the author of *Afraid of All the Things*. She also writes a regular column for *ParentLife* Magazine and enjoys speaking to women around the country about the freedom and rest available in Jesus. Scarlet lives in Middle Tennessee, where she loves sign language with her daughters, nachos by herself, writing for her friends, and learning how to raise ducks with her husband for no reason other than cuteness.

ACKNOWLEDGMENTS

I'm thankful for God, who rescued me from the never-satisfying, always-heartbreaking pursuit of finding my worth in my looks, accomplishments, and the opinions of people.

Thank you, Brandon. You are, hands down, my favorite thing in the world. I've loved you for a long time now, and it's been the easiest thing ever because you're the best. Thank you for being selfless when I'm selfish, compassionate when I'm hard, silly when I'm sobbing, and for cheering me on. I know it's no small thing to have a husband who encourages and supports my dreams and edits my books before they get sent to editors. Thank you for supporting our family and loving our little girls. You're an impossibly good human. Thank you for leading us so well.

Thank you to my babies. Ever, thank you for playing with your sisters and being my helper while I typed at my desk. I loved bouncing ideas off of you, my big girl. Thank you for giving me permission to share some of your stories here to help young girls look to Jesus. I'm honored to be your mommy. Dewy, thank you for holding my neck while

I wrote and edited this book. I love watching you grow up. You are so sweet and so fun, and I just love the way God made you—so special and perfect for this family! Joy, you, my dear, have changed Mommy in a million ways. I remember the first video I saw of you, from when you were still in China. I could tell that you were sweet and gentle, and I didn't know much else. Then God let us go get you and bring you home, and you are just such a joy to parent. You are funny and patient and so kind to others. I am so proud of the beautiful, resilient girl you are.

Thank you to the whole team at B&H, specifically, Michelle (Burke) Freeman! Michelle, you made my dreams come true, and you have become such a source of encouragement in my life. I can't believe I get to do this, and I can't believe I've gotten to do it with you. Thanks for lunches out and for coming to the farm to hang with me and my chickens (may they rest in peace) and my chaotic crew! I've loved getting to know you and work with you.

Thank you to my big, beautiful family, for loving me and being so supportive. I'm so thankful for you.

Special thanks to my sister, Aubrey, my baby biscuit. You were around when I was a teen girl doing absolutely everything the wrong way. We got through it! I love getting to be grown-up friends with you. Thank you for giving me so much grace and being a little sister my girls and I look up to!

Thank you, Katie, Jana, and Caroline. I know I'm not the easiest to love, and y'all have taught me so much about friendship. Nicole and Christy—love and hugs and please move to Tennessee. I will never stop asking—in books, on billboards, whatever it takes :). I miss you and will love you forever.

Thank you, Josh Howerton, for being our pastor and one of our most favorite family friends. Sitting under your teaching has changed my worldview and my heart. Thanks for loving my Brandon so well and for lending me your girls so often.

Brent Ketring, thank you so much for taking the time to look over some of these pages and for giving me your expert advice!

And a special thank you to some of the young ladies in my life. Kelsie, Steph, Parker, Caroline, Anna, Selena—thank you for taking care of and loving my babies when I was away at meetings, or away on a date, or away picking up moving boxes. I love that my girls have such strong, smart, sweet role models.

And to my daughters' sweet girlfriends, Eliana, Amberlee, Anabelle, and Annabelle. I love you girls so much. I love getting to watch you all grow into the beautiful young ladies the Lord made you to be. I pray these words bless you, whether you're reading them now or a few years down the road. I pray they point you to the only One who will satisfy your longings for beauty and security. You girls are special to me, and I'm *way* proud of you.

NOTES

1. Rick Warren, *The Purpose Driven Life* (Grand Rapids: Zondervan, 2002), 148.

2. Jonathan C. Edwards, "Your Marriage Is Not about You," Desiring God, February 23, 2017, https://www.desiringgod.org/articles/your-marriage-is-not-about-you.

3. C. S. Lewis, *Mere Christianity*, rev. and enl. ed. (New York: HarperOne, 2015), 196.